To:

....

From:

....

Date:

....

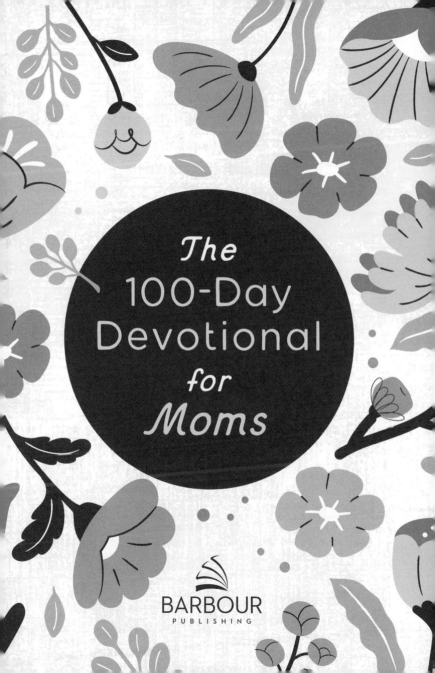

The 100-Day Devotional *for* Moms

BARBOUR
PUBLISHING

© 2025 by Barbour Publishing, Inc.

ISBN 979-8-89151-049-4

Some text previously published as *3-Minute Devotions for Moms.*

Additional content written by Luisa Collopy.

Our mission is to inspire the world with the life-changing message of the Bible.

Member of the
Evangelical Christian
Publishers Association

Printed in China.

Introduction

We are forever changed the moment we become a mom. Life is no longer just about us, our desires, or our dreams. A new piece of us has been brought into the world. . .and it stays with us forever.

Motherhood is the most rewarding, but challenging, job we'll ever have. And we cannot do it alone.

These devotions are especially for those days when you need a bit of encouragement and a reminder of how our relationship with our children often mirrors our relationship with God. Three minutes from your busy day is all you'll need to refresh yourself enough to keep going.

- Read the day's Bible verse and reflect on its meaning
- Read the devotion and think about its application for you
- Pray

Although these devotions aren't meant as a tool for deep Bible study, they can be a touchstone to keep you grounded and focused on God. May every moment you spend with this book remind you what a great calling motherhood truly is.

• •

CHILDREN ARE A BLESSING
AND A GIFT FROM THE LORD.
PSALM 127:3 CEV

Let us run with perseverance the race marked out for us, fixing our eyes on Jesus, the pioneer and perfecter of faith.

HEBREWS 12:1-2 NIV

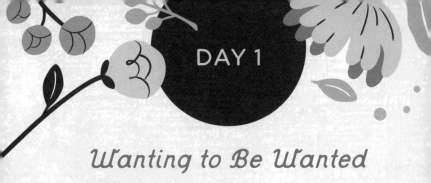

Wanting to Be Wanted

*God remembered Rachel and answered her pleading
and made it possible for her to have children.*
GENESIS 30:22 AMPC

Some women are surprised by pregnancy and motherhood, but others take conscious steps in that direction, whether we spend time reading pregnancy books, eliminating caffeine, or making other changes in anticipation of the day that home pregnancy test reads positive. No matter how long we wait for that day, one thing is certain: we all look forward to greeting a little person we can call our own.

There is, in fact, nothing else that can fill that motherhood void. It's an important part of a woman's makeup, intended to motivate us to propagate the human race. It's deep and sacred and God-given. It allows us to look far beyond the temporary inconvenience, the aches and pains, and the changes to our bodies and to dream big for a child who has not even been born.

God has that same kind of maternal longing for us. He created us, named us, and dreams big dreams for us. He can't wait to shower us with His love and care. Like a mother, God loves completely, forgives instantly, and wants only the best for us. He looked beyond the pain and suffering of seeing His own

Son, Jesus, dying on the cross in order to bring us eternal life.

We all have days when we feel unwanted or unloved, but God gives us a perfect reminder of how untrue that is. The next time that mindset strikes, let's take a few minutes to remember how eager we were to become moms and how much we loved our children before they were even born. Then let's multiply that desire to a level beyond what we can imagine, and we'll start to grasp how much God loves and wants us.

• •

Lord, thank You for loving me and wanting me to be Yours. Thank You too for fulfilling my desire to be a mom. Help me to always find ways to show my children how much they're loved and wanted. Amen.

God's Help Needed

My help comes from the LORD, Who made heaven and earth.
PSALM 121:2 AMP

As moms, we are eager to help our children in innumerable ways from the day they're born, but quickly we move from helping to teaching our children so that they can take care of themselves one day. But as we encourage them in that direction, we have an important "flip side" lesson to teach: the fine line between being self-sufficient and understanding when and how they need to ask for help, especially from God.

The world often tells us that asking for help is wrong or a sign of weakness. As we grow closer to God, however, we know that nothing could be further from the truth. God repeatedly tells us through the Bible to turn to Him for help and let Him help shoulder our burdens.

Some of the most important kings over Israel, such as David and Asa, were men who understood that they could not carry their burdens alone. They asked for God's help personally and sometimes directed their subjects to ask for God's help on their behalf because they knew better than to rely on anything else (see Psalm 54 and 106; 2 Chronicles 14:11 and 20:4). No situation was too small to bring before God.

God doesn't expect us to stumble through life alone—He wants to help us. Although we might not be overseeing kingdoms or making world-changing decisions every day, our situations are always important enough to merit God's help.

Let's teach our children that being self-sufficient can take us far but that we'll only get to a certain point on our own. Showing that we recognize our need and aren't ashamed to ask for God's help can be one of the best lessons we'll ever give as a mom.

• •

Dear God, I don't want to be one of those women who gets so caught up in doing things myself that I forget to ask for help, especially from You. Thank You for always being ready to help me or my children whenever we ask. Amen.

Let God's Wisdom Take Over

The wisest of women builds her house,
but folly with her own hands tears it down.
PROVERBS 14:1 ESV

An interesting headline read JUDGE ORDERS BABY TO BE CUT IN HALF! This verdict was given when King Solomon was approached by two mothers fighting over one living child. These two women, living in the same house by themselves, gave birth to sons three days apart. Here is the account: "'And this woman's son died in the night, because she lay on him. And she arose at midnight and took my son from beside me, while your servant slept, and laid him at her breast, and laid her dead son at my breast. When I rose in the morning to nurse my child, behold, he was dead. But when I looked at him closely in the morning, behold, he was not the child that I had borne.' But the other woman said, 'No, the living child is mine, and the dead child is yours.' The first said, 'No, the dead child is yours, and the living child is mine'" (1 Kings 3:19–22 ESV).

Some of us may find—or have found—ourselves in child custody battles. We know our statements to be true, yet the long-drawn legal process, including the occasional heated arguments and sometimes broken justice system, wears us

down. A judge can issue a not-so-sympathetic judgment saying, "Divide the living child in two, and give half to the one and half to the other" (1 Kings 3:25 ESV). And the sad reality begins with our children splitting the week, going back and forth between two homes.

Some of us will come to the hard decision of giving up shared custody for our children's sake and may end up only with limited holidays to spend with them. If we stand by God's truth and believe that He can and will continue to build His wisdom within us, God will take over our fight. And one day, we might just hear the verdict "Give the child to the mother!"

• •

Lord, please spare my child from more brokenness. Help me to look to You for wisdom, knowing full well that You alone have the best interests at heart for each one of us. I know that You will make all things beautiful again. . .in Your time.

By Any Name

He will be named Wonderful Counselor,
Mighty God, Eternal Father, Prince of Peace.
Isaiah 9:6 hcsb

Mommy. Mama. Mom. Mother.

No matter which name our children choose for us—and even if the name changes during the day, depending on the circumstances—its meaning is the same as the others. Every version of *Mom* represents the kind of love, safety, and human connection that can only be found between us and our children.

The same is true for our connection with God. He holds many titles and fills many roles for us: creator (see Genesis 1:27), protector (see Psalm 91), teacher (see John 14:26), and guide (see Psalm 119:105), just to name a few. But even if our view of God changes because of our circumstances, God Himself never changes. We can rely on Him to be exactly what we need to get through any situation, no matter how difficult.

God is our comforter and healer when we're sick, our guide when we aren't sure which way to turn, and our most enthusiastic cheerleader when we have something to celebrate. He's the one person in the ever-changing (and ever-challenging) world around us that we can always count on—no matter what name

we call Him. It might be *Yahweh, Jehovah, Father,* or something very personal, but regardless of what name we choose, He is always ready to help us when we call on Him.

Our relationships with our children are broad and complex. Our children are growing and changing day by day. As a parent, we adapt to those changes throughout the years. So it is for us as God's children. No matter how much we grow and change throughout our lives, He is always able to provide us with anything and everything we might ever need. In the process, He teaches us how to be all our children need.

• •

Dear Lord, You take on so many different roles for me in every situation, it's hard to keep track. Thank You for being anything and everything I ever need. Amen.

Rules and Regulations

Teach your children right from wrong,
and when they are grown they will still do right.
PROVERBS 22:6 CEV

Theories and opinions on the best ways to raise children abound. Parents might be classified as authoritarian (where children "are seen and not heard"), authoritative ("tough love" with more flexible rules), indulgent (allowing children to make up the rules), or empathetic (basic parenting on the child's emotional state), just to name a few.

Having so many different approaches to the same job can overwhelm us until we understand that there isn't always "one best way" to parent day in and day out. Sometimes the parenting style can change based on our children or the situation. When we aren't sure which tactic is best, it's reassuring to know that God's advice to us about parenting is easily found in the Bible—and this wisdom never changes.

Some instructions deal specifically with raising our children, such as teaching them about God (see Proverbs 22:6 and Deuteronomy 6:7) and following God's rules instead of our own emotions (Ephesians 6:4). Other instructions are directed to our children, reminding them to respect and obey

their parents (Ephesians 6:1–3).

The Bible also includes advice on how to treat everyone around us, which includes our children. We're told to deal with them honestly, treat them the way we'd like to be treated ourselves, and help carry each other's burdens.

Perhaps the best parenting tactic can be summed up by the advice to love each other because God loves us (see 1 John 4:7). Focusing on love and reminding our children how much we love them can point us to the best way to handle any situation. We could say that regardless of which style of parenting we choose, love is the lubricant that allows us to deal with our children day after day.

• •

Dear Lord, sometimes I'm really not sure of the best way to parent my kids. Thank You for what You teach about how I should do the job. Please show me the best way to handle things each day. Amen.

From Power Suit to Sweatpants

Her children stand and bless her.
PROVERBS 31:28 NLT

In the busyness of our careers, we send our kids to daycares and line up babysitters. Progress reports are given to us regularly—as if we are executives requiring an analytics team to create strategies on how to manage our children! So when a young woman decided to be a full-time mom and stepped away from her career, she admitted to going through a personal crisis.

The opposite happened when Mary fully understood what the angel said about her bringing God's Son into the world. She told the angel, "I am the Lord's servant" (Luke 1:38 NLT). After Jesus was born and the shepherds came to worship, sharing how an angel appeared and told them about their Messiah, "Mary treasured up all these things and pondered them in her heart" (Luke 2:19 NIV).

Traveling to Jerusalem for the purification rites, Mary, Joseph, and baby Jesus were met by Simeon, who praised God for Jesus, the salvation promised to Israel. When they met Anna the prophetess, she gave thanks to God and spoke of Jesus as the

redemption of Israel. When Jesus was twelve and His parents left Jerusalem after the Passover, Jesus stayed behind. Going back to look for Him, they found Him among the teachers in the temple court. After Jesus' parents told Him how anxious they had been for the last three days, Jesus answered, "Why were you searching for me?... Didn't you know I had to be in my Father's house?" (Luke 2:49 NIV). Then going to Nazareth from there to raise Jesus, who was an obedient son, "[Mary] treasured all these things in her heart" (v. 51 NIV).

Mary fully embraced her responsibility when she said yes to being Jesus' mother. She was around to hear every good word said about her son. She witnessed His glorious moments from the time He was born until His last days on earth.

Making a choice to leave a career to stay home and care for our children—trading our power suit for sweatpants—will prove to be a big blessing of glorious moments too!

• •

Heavenly Father, thank You for the privilege of being a mother. Help me to understand this important role and how I can best fulfill it.

Far-Reaching Dreams

To him who is able to do far more abundantly than all that we ask or think, according to the power at work within us, to him be glory.
EPHESIANS 3:20–21 ESV

It's common for us to dream about our unborn children, working out questions as we sleep. Will this child be a girl or boy? Who will this new little person look like, act like? How will he or she deal with life? Even in our waking moments, we wonder if our child will have a sense of humor, a love of music, or a connection with the outdoors.

Once our babies are born, we continue to dream. Hair and eyes are now known, but as our children begin to develop their distinct personalities and interests, we start to dream for them rather than about them. We imagine the friends they will have. We see them sitting at the piano during recitals and wonder if a professional musician could be in the works. We see a love and compassion for animals and know those characteristics would be important for a veterinarian. We spot dexterity in the kitchen and imagine a head chef in the making.

While we are dreaming for our children, God is dreaming too. No doubt He was the first to see our potential to be good

moms. He also sees the gifts He has placed in us growing and taking shape. But unlike us, God sees all—from the beginning to the end. He knows how to inspire us to keep moving toward His best for us. He sees the obstacles in the path and shows us how to overcome them.

Let's aim high for our children and dream big dreams for them. But let's also dare to dream along with God for the fulfillment of our gifts and callings. What could be a better course for our lives than to live as God dreams we will?

• •

Dear Lord, it's easy for me to get caught up in setting goals and enjoying dreams, but I know You've mapped out the ultimate plan for my children and for me. Thank You for those special plans, whatever they are. Show me how to follow You in that direction. Amen.

Always Interested

*An intelligent heart acquires knowledge,
and the ear of the wise seeks knowledge.*
PROVERBS 18:15 ESV

One mom in the neighborhood has always been a no-frills tomboy, but all the girls know she paints the most creative fingernails on their street. Her neighbor doesn't care for football but can recite all the Heisman Trophy winners in a flash. Another used to claim that trying to understand the stock market gave her a headache, but now she can hold her own in any conversation about trends and projections. What pointed these women in directions they would have never chosen for themselves? Their children.

Of course, this happened because their children had different interests than their own. When our interests agree, it's easy to share the journey of discovery, but when our interests aren't the same—and they often aren't because God has created each of us uniquely—it is tempting to simply sign our children up for an activity of their choice and let it go at that. But by doing that, we would miss the opportunity to explore something new together, learning that specific interest and also growing in relationship with each other.

Few things get children as excited—or eager to talk—as sharing about their hobbies, favorite sports, or other pastimes. And what a precious glimpse we can get into our children's lives as we spend time together.

Let's thank God for all the things that make our children unique, even if it means their interests don't match up with ours. Those differences can actually be the starting point for something wonderful between us. And in so doing, we are following Christ's example. He, the mighty Son of God, left heaven and concerned Himself with human interests in order to bind Himself in relationship with us.

• •

Dear Lord, I'm glad my child has so many interests, even those that might not appeal very much to me. Help us find common ground and enjoy learning from each other. Amen.

The Making of a Titan

*Let each generation tell its children of your
mighty acts; let them proclaim your power.*
PSALM 145:4 NLT

Jocelyn was named one of the titans in her industry. When
she was interviewed for a magazine feature, she credited her
mother, who, as a top executive, took her to work during her
school breaks. She remembered playing under the desk while
her mom made decisions and handled her team. She learned
about courage, resilience, and empathy from her mother.

As mothers, we have the greatest influence in our children's
lives. They often come to us with their tears and fears, with
their physical hurt and emotional pains. We are their sounding
boards. We are their first responders. How we handle each
learning moment is up to us.

After the deaths of Naomi's husband and sons, she advised
her daughters-in-law, Orpah and Ruth, to go back to their families. Orpah said her goodbye and left. But Ruth saw something
worthy in Naomi, her mother-in-law, and wanted to stay. She
said, "Wherever you go, I will go; wherever you live, I will live.
Your people will be my people, and your God will be my God.
Wherever you die, I will die, and there I will be buried. May

24

the LORD punish me severely if I allow anything but death to separate us!" (Ruth 1:16–17 NLT). Ruth, a Moabite, would have worshipped the god Chemosh, not the God of Abraham, Isaac, and Jacob. But she saw Naomi's faith in the one true God and desired it for herself.

In the New Testament, Eunice, Timothy's mother, lived out her faith from the heart (2 Timothy 1:5). As a result, Timothy had a strong personal relationship with his Maker and became a spiritual titan, charged with caring for the church by the apostle Paul.

Our hope for our children is for them to grow into responsible adults who are in love with Jesus. Living out our faith in Christ and obeying Him is the best gift to leave our children. Let's think about our spiritual legacies.

* * * * * * * * * * * * * * * * * *

Father, help me to live my life in a way that's honoring to You. When I forget to walk the talk, let the Holy Spirit convict me and quickly turn me around.

Mom's To-Do List

Many are the plans in a person's heart,
but it is the LORD's purpose that prevails.
PROVERBS 19:21 NIV

Whether we keep a running list on our smartphones, stash a notepad in our purses, or jot reminders on whatever scrap of paper is available, each tactic serves the same purpose: keeping our Mom "to-do" list at the top of our minds so that we don't miss something important.

Oftentimes, the demands of the day dictate what's on that list. (Buying the things our child needs to complete a school project or picking up groceries so that our family can eat dinner are examples.) But there may be a few items we can add to the list that will allow us to help others and let them know that God loves and cares for them.

Adding a few God items might be easier than we think. For example, we could pick up some extra canned vegetables or boxed dinner mixes for the local food pantry. Better yet, maybe we could volunteer to help there sometimes. We could run an errand for someone who is housebound because of age, illness, or injury. We might send an encouraging card to someone we know who is going through a difficult time. It's easy to imagine

that God would love to see things like these on our lists.

Let's ask God if we need to cut something from our to-do lists or juggle our tasks so that we can make a few God items a priority. If we don't make a conscious effort, our day-to-day circumstances will keep us maxed out, and we'll miss the blessing that comes with helping others. After all, God was tending the universe when He stopped to make time for us. Shouldn't we follow His example?

· ·

Dear Lord, I can get so wrapped up in the things that need to be done that I forget to be sure I'm putting Your priorities first. Show me where my list needs to change so that it matches what You want me to do. Amen.

The Small Jobs

*And whatever you do, whether in word or deed,
do it all in the name of the Lord Jesus,
giving thanks to God the Father through him.*
COLOSSIANS 3:17 NIV

Sweeping cereal from every corner of the kitchen. Changing race car sheets at 3 a.m. Searching through every drugstore in town for a certain type of hairbrush. Checking the minutes left on our family's cellular account. Scheduling dentist appointments. . .

They aren't big jobs, and many times we handle them without rating a "thank you" from family members. But these jobs are the makings of normal life for us moms and can accumulate until some days we feel that all our time is spent on "little" stuff. It's time for us to remember that God doesn't look at it like that.

When we are taking care of our families, we are literally doing God's work. Each task is important, even though it may seem at times to be menial in nature. You might also be able to enhance the work by adding a spiritual element. One mother keeps photos of her children clipped to her car visor and prays for each of them while she's running errands. Another thanks God for a different blessing every time she picks up something

and moves it to the right spot in her home. And yet another mom cranks up her favorite praise music while she vacuums or dusts.

Those mundane jobs take on new meaning when we see every load of laundry, sink of dirty dishes, trip to the market, dental appointment, vacuumed floor, and dinner casserole as a way to serve God by serving our families. What ministry wields more influence and produces more obvious results? God holds every facet of motherhood in high esteem, and our days will take on renewed meaning when we see it that way as well.

• •

Lord, it can be easy to look down on the little jobs of motherhood and think they don't really matter. But everything I do as a mom is important to You and to my family. Help me to remember that, no matter what I spend my time doing. Amen.

When Your Body Starts Saying "Stop!"

*Don't you realize that all of you together are the temple
of God and that the Spirit of God lives in you?*
1 Corinthians 3:16 nlt

Did you notice that the Stop sign at the end of the street had become blurrier? How about feeling achier than usual after your Zumba class? It seems like we have failing body parts—eyes, ankles, and more—as we celebrate milestone birthdays starting at forty. Somehow, our bodies no longer agree with our usual activities and routines, saying, "Stop! I want to quit!" Whatever is happening, our bodies seem on a decline. *Are we just going to give up?*

As God's daughters, we need to remember the apostle Paul's words to the Corinthians: "We never give up. Though our bodies are dying, our spirits are being renewed every day." (2 Corinthians 4:16 nlt).

Aging will happen no matter how many nips and tucks we have or how many marathons we run or how many rigid diets we try. We hear of new technologies that can help prolong life—we might even test them for ourselves—but we will still come

to the end of life. We should not fear aging and death. Instead, we need to be completely honest with ourselves because we don't want to disfigure ourselves if we keep on fighting age with unnecessary methods.

We can gracefully accept the aging process by reframing our thoughts. Drinking more water and getting eight hours of sleep will bring better health. Walking and going outdoors to breathe fresh air and to enjoy the beauty of God's creation can change our moods. Most importantly, feeding our souls with God's Word, prayer, music, and times of rest with God will surely build up our faith and spiritual life—the most important part of our fitness routine!

● ●

Though my body is not what it used to be,
Lord, help me to celebrate it and to take
care of it in a God-honoring way.

Our Fortress

Our LORD and our God, you are my
mighty rock, my fortress, my protector.
2 SAMUEL 22:2 CEV

Rare indeed is the adult who can't look back and remember building a fort. It's a classic childhood pastime. In the mind of a child, blankets and cushions draped across the furniture might be seen as protection from a sibling's attack, a place to hide from imaginary enemies, or even an indoor camping spot. As adults, we outgrow the blanket-and-cushion version of a protective fortress, but we find the same needed security for ourselves and our families in other types of forts.

A bigger paycheck can mean a larger home in a nicer neighborhood. Money in the bank or a higher number of stock shares can cover our children's college education or fund our retirement. Sending our children to particular schools can expose them to a better environment or opportunities they might not have otherwise.

Whether by a real-life reality check or increased wisdom as we age, we usually figure out something about these newer forts. In the long run they don't protect us any better than our children's blankets over the dining room table did. They slide

and fall, leaving us vulnerable and in search of answers.

God is our fortress and protector. He is our most secure foundation and the best defense against any attack from our enemy, Satan. We can't keep an eye on our children twenty-four hours a day, but God can. We can't guarantee there will always be money in the bank, but God can meet all our needs. God is the only one who can keep us truly safe in this unpredictable world.

Rather than relying on a mom-made fort for protection, let's ask God to help us trust Him to do the job and teach our children to do the same.

• •

Dear God, the world tries to convince me that material things can keep my family safe, but I know that's not true. You are the real protector and the only one I can trust. Thank You for being my fortress. Amen.

Beautiful Enough

Charm can be deceiving, and beauty fades away, but a woman who honors the LORD deserves to be praised.
PROVERBS 31:30 CEV

The world's version of beauty stares at us from every direction. Magazines, movies, and other media products flaunt models with flowing hair, knockout smiles, and sculpted figures. Although we know the pictures aren't true to life, we can't always stop ourselves from falling into the comparison trap. It's a game we are destined to lose because we all fall short of those computer-enhanced versions of beauty.

As we strive to be comfortable with our physical appearance, let's not forget that our children—both sons and daughters—are fighting the same battle. Our desire is to build our children's confidence whenever and however we can. The challenge lies in learning how to compliment their physical appearances without having it backfire—either because they become vain or (more likely) because they don't believe what we say.

Many times, our children reject our comments about their beauty because we're Mom and we're *supposed* to see their beauty. But more often it's because none of us truly believes we're beautiful until we see ourselves through God's eyes.

God always looks beneath the skin straight to our hearts and souls. What He finds is a wonderful creation that is unique in every way, a person who is trying to be more like Him every day. And that's beautiful.

When we ask God to help us see ourselves like He does, we'll discover treasures that we never imagined. The more we learn to appreciate those treasures and shine from the inside out, the more beautiful we become to ourselves and to others.

Sure, it would be nice to look like that cover model. But having a beauty that's covered with God is one of the most valuable examples we can ever show our children.

• •

Lord, thank You for the wonderful creation I am. Help me to love myself for what's on the inside, not based on what I see in the mirror. Then teach me how to instill the same perspective in my children. Amen.

The Power of "We"

Let us not neglect our meeting together, as some people do.
HEBREWS 10:25 NLT

Summer breaks and holidays often seem to interrupt fellowship. One woman could not help but comment on how much she misses her Bible study. *Do you feel the same when your study group is on hiatus?*

A small group of moms has been meeting on Fridays for close to a decade. Some are retired. Some are stay-at-home moms, while some are in the workforce. Although their ages vary and they go to different churches, their close bond was formed over their love for God's Word and one another.

It is no secret that women thrive on fellowship. Being in a community helps us to remember that we are not alone, that we can make lifelong connections. Fellowship helps us remain encouraged and strong as we find acceptance and a safe place in our groups.

In Hebrews we read, "Let us think of ways to motivate one another to acts of love and good works. And let us not neglect our meeting together, as some people do, but encourage one another, especially now that the day of his return is drawing near" (10:24–25 NLT). Notice that we ought to show acts of love

and good works. "Are any of you suffering hardships?" James wrote. "You should call for the elders of the church to come and pray over you" (James 5:13–14 NLT). Mixing action with prayer is even more powerful in encouraging the body of Christ, as we are told to "love each other with genuine affection" (Romans 12:10 NLT). Imagine what would happen if we happily baked cookies and prepared casseroles not just as part of the meal trains and potlucks we sign up for but as a thankful surprise for the blessing of friendships.

Our "we" time is powerful and important! A Bible study group is one venue that provides spiritual encouragement and growth. Just like what the Bible described, we can "[devote ourselves] to the [Word of God], and to fellowship, and to sharing in meals (including the Lord's Supper), and to prayer" (Acts 2:42 NLT). Let's get our Bible studies up and running!

• •

What a blessing, Lord, to be in the
company of women who love You!
Help us to be grateful that we can belong!

37

Finally Saying "Yes"

*"I know the plans I have for you," declares the
Lord, "plans to prosper you and not to harm
you, plans to give you hope and a future."*
JEREMIAH 29:11 NIV

We all have days when it seems like the word we say to our children most frequently is "no." Whatever the situation might be, the necessary "no" can be painful for both of us because, as parents, we want to give our children many good things. When the requests go against what we know is best, however, we must say the dreaded word—maybe repeatedly—and encourage our children to adjust and move on.

Although our children don't always realize it, we aren't the only ones doling out "no" these days. Sometimes God gives it to us as well. We've all prayed for something we thought would be good and heard God's "no" through circumstances. At those times, our disappointment and frustration can mount, especially when it concerns something we've hoped and planned for.

At those times, we should ask ourselves if what we've asked for is a good thing or a God thing. Some things may be good for others, but God knows they are not good for us. When He says

38

no, we can be sure that He doesn't see us as one of many but as one in particular, with specific needs and personal purpose. Our wisdom is limited, and we have no knowledge of what lies ahead. What might seem good from our perspective may not fit into God's bigger plan for our lives.

It can be difficult to regroup after God's "no." But just as we teach our children, we need to accept the "no" and move on, even if we don't understand the reason. Because even if we don't know where we're going, we can be confident that God does—and every "no" He says points us back toward a "yes."

• •

Lord, I want a lot of things that seem good, but You know what's really best. Help me to accept when You tell me no. Change my heart so that I want the same things You do. Thank You for the plans You have for me. Amen.

Fixing Our Eyes

*We do this by keeping our eyes on Jesus,
the champion who initiates and perfects our faith.*
HEBREWS 12:2 NLT

"Hold my hand, and I'll help you." "Don't look down, just watch me." "We're not lost, I know where we're going." It probably would be hard for us to count the number of times we've said those phrases or similar ones to our children. We start teaching them at a young age that they can trust us in any situation. We'll guide them where they need to be and help them do what they need to do—if they'll just let us.

The same is true for God's role in our lives. God is always ready to instruct us, guide us, and show us the right direction. We only have to ask and trust, though doing that on a regular basis can be tough. Some days, life is so hard that the desire for different circumstances nearly consumes us. On other days, we walk with confidence in ourselves and our lives because things are rosy and our loved ones are healthy and happy.

When should we fix our sights on God? At both extremes and all in between. People come and go, circumstances change, and life is never the same for long. What's wonderful today might be horrible tomorrow, and vice versa.

Fixing our eyes too much on any of it can warp our perspective and send us spiraling toward depression or leave us with a cocky attitude. Fixing our eyes on the one constant in life—God—can keep us grounded and able to face any situation because we know we're not alone.

We must accept God's guidance in our lives just as certainly as we expect our children to accept our guidance. Like any good parent, He's always waiting to point us in the right direction. And He is always the best guide of all.

• •

Dear God, thank You for being the constant guide in my life, whether things seem good or bad. Remind me to always ask for Your help, and teach me how to trust that You're right beside me. Amen.

Learning Conflict Resolutions from Mom

*She opens her mouth with wisdom,
and the teaching of kindness is on her tongue.*
PROVERBS 31:26 ESV

One mom's twins are arguing again about why they couldn't have been single births so that they could have their own birthdays. Another mom's daughters, very close in age, are fighting over a sweater they each would like to wear to school. Still, another's sons each want to borrow the family car for a drive to the movies. . .alone. Well, we know how it is to have a household of children—all with different personalities!

Mom is normally tasked with handling such conflicts. We often hear, "Mom! They're annoying me!" Even if we want our kids to handle the issue, we find ourselves stepping in to prevent the argument from escalating to World War III. So we lovingly listen to the complaints and try to sift through the emotions to get to the bottom of the problem. Sometimes we are successful in making both parties happy; sometimes we are not. But our goal is always the same: resolve the conflict.

Can you believe how effective the leadership of a mom is

when it comes to conflict resolution! Mom's listening ear will often alleviate some tension. It is good for us moms to remember Proverbs 18:13 (ESV): "If one gives an answer before he hears, it is his folly and shame."

Mom is also good at navigating through an acceptable and workable solution between opposing parties to help repair the fallout. Proverbs 31:26 (ESV) says, "She opens her mouth with wisdom, and the teaching of kindness is on her tongue." A mom can draw out what's deep in the hearts of those in conflict and help them decide on the best course of action to put in place.

Mom, how wonderful that you can be instrumental in building an environment of connection and understanding in the family! Praise God that you can prevent rumblings and help keep peace at home!

• •

Help me, Lord, to be the peacemaker
You have called me to be, offering
words that will heal and restore!

A Marked Woman

*When you heard the message of truth, the gospel
of your salvation, and when you believed in Him,
you were also sealed with the promised Holy Spirit.*
EPHESIANS 1:13 HCSB

For many of us moms, our bodies are never exactly the same after we go through pregnancy and childbirth. Spider veins, a not-quite-so-tight stomach, and wider, flatter feet can all be everlasting reminders of those nine months—marks that signal our passage to motherhood.

When we learn about Jesus Christ and believe in Him, we are sealed—marked—as belonging to God (see Ephesians 1:13). It's not as obvious as our physical motherhood marks, but it's real just the same. It's an invisible mark that shows itself through our actions and attitudes.

What kinds of actions? A contemporary Christian song in the late 1990s went through a list of things people sometimes use to show their Christianity: a cross necklace, a BLESSINGS welcome mat at the door, a fish magnet on the car. Those are outward symbols meant for the world to see, but they aren't true markings (which was the point of the song).

The real ways we show that we love and follow God are what

other people might consider insignificant or weak. We close our mouths and walk away instead of saying what we'd like. We point out when the cashier gives us extra change and return it. We take extra pencils and paper to school for children who can't afford to buy their own. Quiet things like these often speak louder than any flashing signs or messaged T-shirts because they show our true character. People learn about God not only through the things we say but also through the things we do day in and day out.

There are many ways people can see God's invisible mark of ownership on us through our actions and attitudes. That's where our true influence lies.

• •

Lord, I know that I belong to You, but the world needs to know it too. I want to be a marked woman for You. Help me to find ways to show that I'm Yours so that people around me will want the same thing for themselves. Amen.

Wants and Needs

*My God will supply all your needs according
to His riches in glory in Christ Jesus.*
PHILIPPIANS 4:19 HCSB

"You're old enough for your wants not to hurt you" is a phrase
sometimes heard during childhood. It's usually said by an adult
when children whine about not getting their way, whether
they want a new puppy or to make up their own rules instead
of following ours. They're asking for something that the adult
believes is a want, not a need.

We can easily see the difference between wants and needs
when we're the parent teaching our child. It's not always so
obvious, however, or as easy to accept when we're the person
with a "want." The world's version of what's important to do,
to have, or to want often differs from what God says is important. Even when we love God and try to follow His teachings,
we can fall into the trap of thinking we need things that really
are better classified as "wants."

God gives us everything we need: food, shelter, clothing,
love. Then God goes beyond that by blessing us with many other
things that we don't necessarily need but that we want: another
car for the family, a larger home in a nicer neighborhood, the

funds to pay for a vacation or our children's activities.

There's nothing wrong with wanting nice things for ourselves or our family, especially if the desire coincides with God's plan. Having a larger home might give us the space to host an exchange student. Allowing our child to join a different gymnastics program could lead to better opportunities later.

The thing to remember is that wants and needs are all about perspective, whether we're looking at our own or our child's. When we ask God for His perspective, He'll help us know which is which.

• •

Lord, You know how hard it can be to focus on what I really need instead of just what I want. Teach me to do better with knowing the difference so that I can also teach it to my children. Amen.

Unpacking Memories

Good people are remembered long after they are gone.
PROVERBS 10:7 CEV

A son finally emptied the storage unit and brought home his late mom's sealed boxes a year after her passing. Opening a couple of the boxes, he found his mom's magazine collection, all dating back to his childhood days. Browsing through the magazines, he found recipes his mom lovingly prepared when he was growing up—and the memory of the aromas of his mom's cooking brought him back to their dinner table in their old family home.

When we are long gone, what memories will our children unpack? Will they be the delectable dishes—the holiday pot roast with the secret ingredient—that we will pass on like a family heirloom? Will it be the miniature tea set that we lovingly dust today, hoping that it will find its way to our daughter's home one day?

We all have our quirks and character and flaws and influences as we walk this earth. And when we pass on, we leave behind some unique memories. They will represent who we are—a great cook, the knickknack collector, and more. They will show what we offer—a great listener, a fabulous decorator,

etc. They will also reveal our flaws—always late, anxious, and so on. No matter what will be unpacked of us later, it will be the reality that we are no longer around. . .just a memory.

Unpacking memories is like going through a treasure box that contains both beautiful and painful experiences. Life is a mixture of contradictions. But one thing is for sure: "Good people are remembered long after they are gone."

While we're still able to take stock of our lives, let's sort through what does not add value to our legacies. We can let go of the hurts, burdens, and negativity to make room for a heart full of love and hope. Once we have purged our unwanted baggage, let's lovingly pack our "boxes" with joyful remembrances that will bring smiles to our children when their time to unpack comes.

• •

Heavenly Father, help me to be intentional in living a fulfilled life in Your Son so that I can leave behind the joy of my salvation.

Sharing a Lunch

*"I was hungry and you gave me something to eat,
I was thirsty and you gave me something to drink,
I was a stranger and you invited me in."*
MATTHEW 25:35 NIV

"Your child's lunch account balance has dropped below the acceptable minimum. Please add funds to your child's account."

The email flashed on the computer screen, confusing Anna. She had deposited $20 into both her children's accounts a few weeks earlier, but it was really only there as a buffer. Both kids usually took their lunches, so they only used the accounts occasionally. When she asked her twins about it that afternoon, the answer surprised her more than the email.

"Mom, Jared hasn't been eating lunch. He said his dad lost his job so they don't have money for lunch. We've been taking turns going through the line and getting a tray so we can give it to him. We knew you always have money in our account."

In typical seventh-grade fashion, Anna's children hadn't thought to tell her about the situation. In typical Jesus fashion, they hadn't thought about whether they should help Jared. They simply did it.

Jesus commended those who tuned in to people's needs and

met them however they could and without worrying about what other people thought. He also taught that being kind to those who need help is like being kind to Jesus Himself.

God provides us with everything we need—and often more. If we take the time to look, we could all probably find ways to help feed someone like Anna's children did. Maybe we pick up the tab for the car behind us in the drive-through. Buy some extra things at the grocery store and donate them to a local food pantry. Or surprise a friend with an invitation to dinner. Whatever we choose to do—however big or small—it's sure to brighten that person's day. And ours.

• •

Lord, show me how I can feed or clothe people nearby. Help it to become an automatic response for me and something my children learn to recognize and follow themselves. Amen.

Restful Watching

He will not let your foot slip—he who
watches over you will not slumber.
PSALM 121:3 NIV

No matter how many times we hear it beforehand, nothing truly prepares us for the round-the-clock demands of motherhood. We move from countless diapers and feedings with newborns to continually running behind toddlers to sleepless nights while school projects get finished or teenagers return home safely. The constant vigil continues even when our children move out because they never leave our hearts and minds. We wonder sometimes how we'll push through our exhaustion to the next day. Sometimes it seems we might never experience true rest again.

When those times come, we need to remind ourselves that we weren't meant to be on "active duty" 24-7. God instructs us to rest and find refreshment. We also know that God rested after finishing all of creation. And if God takes time to rest, we certainly should. The trouble is that sometimes when we actually step away, we still fret about what might (or might not) happen. We have trouble letting go and trusting that things will be fine if we're not watching.

Here's a reassurance that should help us in those moments: God is over everything, and God always knows what's happening. One of the psalmists wrote of how God never slumbers or sleeps. In this context, "slumber" refers to nodding off or taking a quick nap as opposed to experiencing deep sleep. God never takes a few minutes off to rest from watching over us. And God certainly never falls asleep.

When we remind ourselves of this and believe that it's true, we are freed to enjoy the rest that can seem so elusive. Here's to taking a deep breath, propping our feet up, and relaxing for a few minutes. God is still watching over things even when we snatch a much-needed nap.

• •

Lord, give me the energy I need to handle each day, but show me when I need to stop and rest. Thank You for never getting tired and needing a break Yourself. Amen.

Withdrawing to a Solitary Life

Turn to me and be gracious to me,
for I am lonely and afflicted.
PSALM 25:16 ESV

Women are social beings by nature. Wherever we are, we like to make connections and keep them going whether by text messaging or following each other on social media. At work, the fifteen-minute coffee break is not long enough, especially on Mondays when we like to exchange stories about our weekends. At home, we want to regale our husbands with the latest news about "everything under the sun" no matter how tired they are.

But this single mom started to withdraw when she became an empty nester. Lifelong friends felt her pull away and were concerned. No phone call or letter or greeting card could persuade her to respond and reconnect. Did she just want her personal space?

Yes, we also need alone time, when we can be comfortable with our own company, our own thoughts. We don't have to tire ourselves by constantly entertaining people and contributing to conversations. Stepping away to relax and enjoy some peace

and quiet by ourselves is good for recharging.

Struggles with isolation will come to us at some point too. Perhaps the stress of something new—a change, such as being an empty nester—is so overwhelming that a temporary break from the company of friends is more welcome than putting on a show. Taking a sabbatical from our normal life seems better than not living up to our or others' expectations.

However, living a solitary life to the point of excluding people we are close to may be a sign of a deeper issue. It's okay to send out an SOS, maybe even seek professional help, to help us function again. And it's also the best time to recognize how much we need God to get us out of our solitude and loneliness. Psalm 25:16–18 (ESV) says, "Turn to me and be gracious to me, for I am lonely and afflicted. The troubles of my heart are enlarged; bring me out of my distresses. Consider my affliction and my trouble, and forgive all my sins."

Yes, Lord, consider my loneliness and affliction right now. Help me to overcome what I am going through. Forgive me for my unrighteousness.

Joyful Noises

*Shout for joy to God, all the earth! "All the
earth bows down to you; they sing praise to
you, they sing the praises of your name."*
PSALM 66:1, 4 NIV

Most children have an innate love of music. Soon after they're
born, babies babble and coo, creating a special music of their
own. It can be such fun to watch them singing and dancing
with abandon, enjoying the moment without caring what
other people think. We laugh and clap along with them,
belt out songs and make goofy motions, acting just as silly. But
it can be hard to keep that open mindset once our children
grow up and we no longer have a built-in excuse for singing
and dancing. We may feel self-conscious or worry that God is
put off by such displays of childlike behavior.

It might help to remember that God gave us the gift of music
to enjoy for ourselves, share with others, and use as a way to
praise Him. It doesn't matter how loudly or softly we sing, how
awkwardly we dance, or how carefully we stay on key. God just
wants us to let the joy in our hearts come through in whatever
way we can manage. He calls us to sing praises all of our days,
not just when we're children or have little ones of our own. We

should still be praising God when our kids are too cool in their own minds to sing out or we're too arthritic to raise our hands.

There is no doubt, the day will come when our children move from their "cool" phase and reach places of deep, heartfelt worship as they grow in their faith. And when we release ourselves to do so, we will rediscover our childlike enjoyment of the gift of music as we continue to praise God by releasing the song in our hearts.

• •

Dear Lord, thank You for the gift of music.
Teach me to enjoy Your songs with the
heart of a child who worships freely
and draws others to You. Amen.

The Makeup Mask

Cleanse me with hyssop, and I will be clean;
wash me, and I will be whiter than snow.
PSALM 51:7 NIV

Our morning routines might change a bit as we go through different phases of motherhood, but one thing usually doesn't get eliminated completely: the cleansing, moisturizing, and makeup ritual. Some days, we might spend twenty minutes or more going through the steps. On others, we feel lucky to splash water on our faces and slap on some foundation and mascara. Either way, we're making an effort to look a little better for the world.

The freshness of color fades and the smooth, even finish disappears by day's end, leaving us with remnants that need to be washed away. We'll start fresh again the next morning, but at bedtime, we're laid bare before ourselves with mirror and glaring lights: natural skin with no makeup to cover blemishes, bags, or other perceived imperfections. We go through the same cycle with the person we present to the world versus the person God knows we are—natural and covered up, over and over.

It can be hard to reveal our true selves to the people around

us. So many other moms seem to have their lives and situations under control. Admitting that we don't can be humbling or downright terrifying, and we don't want to look like a mess. So we put on our public face and only let our closest confidantes glimpse pieces of the truth.

The mask we wear in public doesn't last forever, just like our makeup. It also never hides our true selves from God—and He loves us anyway. Even if we never want to share some things with others, we can come clean with God. Whatever we're facing and however we feel about it, God loves us and can help us through it. We just need to have the courage to be honest with Him.

• •

Lord, the world might expect me to seem perfect and all put together, but I know that You don't. Thank You for loving me no matter what. Give me the courage to be clean and honest with You so that I can get through whatever problems I'm facing. Amen.

Freely Give

*For we brought nothing into the world,
and we cannot take anything out of the world.*
1 TIMOTHY 6:7 ESV

A mother decided to surprise her adult children with gifts of money after a severe illness. But as she continued to recover and regain her normal functions, she started regretting her decision and thought of asking for the money back!

We have been convinced by financial advisers to work past retirement age and to keep saving for it. Everything we do should make good financial sense so that we can keep growing our resources. And once we reach our dream financial health and there is no more fear of possible financial ruin, it's time for us to step back and enjoy life as we planned. Sadly, our physical health may be long gone, and we are no longer able to check items off our bucket list. Our lives have become even more fragile, and the money we worked hard for ends up being earmarked for our medical payments. . .and for someone else to enjoy.

The Bible is very clear though: "For we brought nothing into the world, and we cannot take anything out of the world." Job expressed the same idea as the apostle Paul when he said,

"Naked I came from my mother's womb, and naked shall I return" (Job 1:21 ESV).

The apostle Paul went one step further. He described where the desire to have money leads: "For the love of money is a root of all kinds of evils. It is through this craving that some have wandered away from the faith and pierced themselves with many pangs" (1 Timothy 6:10 ESV). Remember the mother who wanted her gifts back? It's hard to imagine any reasonable excuse to ask someone to return money that you gave and that was received in good faith. Hard feelings are around the corner!

Let's not wait for declining physical health and emotional decision-making to come before we consider what to give away. We all hope for the best lives possible for our children. What a beautiful surprise for them to receive unexpected gifts, especially gifts of money, given wholeheartedly!

• •

Lord, help me to remember that everything belongs to You. What You have blessed me with, remind me to use to bless others!

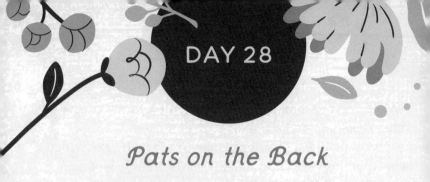

Pats on the Back

A voice from heaven said, "This is my Son,
whom I love; with him I am well pleased."
MATTHEW 3:17 NIV

Each of us has a need for approval and positive feedback, and we moms can become the biggest cheerleaders in our children's lives. Rewards can be as simple as stickers or a piece of candy, or as "grown up" as a later curfew, an expanded phone plan, or spending money for a special occasion. But as much as our children can appreciate the material rewards, our positive words to them might be the best—and most lasting—gift of all.

When Jesus was ready to begin His ministry on earth, He went to the river to be baptized like many other people in the community. Something special happened when Jesus stood up after being immersed, with water dripping from His hair and clothes. A dove flew down and landed on Jesus, and the people heard God speak. God announced that Jesus was His Son and that He loved and was pleased with Him.

Think about that for a minute. The God of the universe proclaimed His satisfaction with Jesus for anyone to hear. There are many lessons to be learned from this, but perhaps the most important is the power of encouragement.

Jesus was fully God but also fully human. The human side of Jesus needed positive reinforcement just like we do. Just like our children do. No matter our age, there's something about hearing "Good job" that can fill a void that few other words can. But sometimes life gets so busy that we forget to stop and say those words to our children.

It might help if we take time to write down some things to encourage our children and give them the list as a tangible reminder of our love and pride. Then, we might want to try doing that for ourselves.

• •

Dear Lord, You are the ultimate encourager for each of us. Thank You for encouraging me when I need it, through family, friends, or other ways. Show me how I can do the same thing for my children in whatever way they need. Amen.

Drive-Through Prayers

Be unceasing in prayer [praying perseveringly].
1 THESSALONIANS 5:17 AMPC

We've all had those days when things are crazy from beginning to end, no matter how hard we try to keep on track. Work is hectic, our family is on a tight schedule for the night, and we get home to realize dinner isn't ready because we forgot to plug in the slow cooker. We want to scream in frustration as we head to the drive-through so that everyone can be fed.

Our prayer life can be the same way. We have days when we're able to enjoy our morning quiet time by reading the Bible or a devotional and spending some time in prayer. Then there are other days when (if we're honest with ourselves) things get hectic and prayer doesn't cross our minds. When a nudge in our day does remind us to pray, we might be so busy that we're not sure how to fit it in.

We have an even greater dilemma when we consider that the Bible teaches that we should pray without ceasing. The chances that we moms can sit and spend an entire day focusing solely on prayer are virtually nonexistent. So how do we pray without ceasing?

Fortunately, prayer isn't an "all or none" proposition in

which we must spend a certain amount of time or meet particular criteria before it counts. God simply wants us to keep an attitude of open communication. That means we might speak with Him as we iron clothes, while waiting for a meeting to start, or as we sit in traffic. The point is to stay connected throughout the day, to leave your heart phone on. Just like you are always happy to hear from your children, God is always happy to hear from you.

• •

Lord, the Bible tells us to pray constantly, not just when we have big blocks of uninterrupted time. Thank You for loving the small, ongoing prayers just as much as something more formal. Fill me with the desire to pray through every part of my day. Amen.

Body-Shaming Can Start with Anyone

There was no sparkle in Leah's eyes,
but Rachel had a beautiful figure and a lovely face.
GENESIS 29:17 NLT

"Ladies and gentlemen, boys and girls! Presenting. . .Mommy and her tummy!" It was a toddler boy who made this loud announcement while he was with his mom, who was trying on some clothes in the dressing room. Embarrassed to go view herself in the common-room mirror after that, the mom decided it was the end of her shopping day. She didn't want to encounter strangers staring at her.

Have you experienced body-shaming? Maybe in your own home your teenage daughter rolled her eyes with disapproval when she saw you wearing your snug-fitting workout clothes because it seemed like you were going to pop out of them. Or maybe it's date night and your husband suggested you change into something else because the outfit doesn't complement your shape like it used to.

How about social media? You posted some photos on your timeline. One was from your recent family trip, and a friend

wrote an "Are you sick?" question. Another photo of the cake you lovingly baked received a laughing emoji and a "Don't stuff your face!" nasty comment from a relative. *What if comments like these are triggers for someone with an eating disorder or guilt and shame over a current weight struggle?*

Whether said in jest or with good intention, such comments can be reckless and hurtful. They send a message of imperfection others see in us that can impact how we, in turn, see ourselves. It's hard enough that we already agonize over how we can regain our physiques of long ago and then subject our bodies to diet fads and exercise regimens. Top that off with unfavorable comments from home and everywhere else and it will be harder to live up to a changing ideal standard.

It's only God's Word that constantly reminds us of how precious we are—and we should be grateful. "Thank you for making me so wonderfully complex! Your workmanship is marvelous—how well I know it" (Psalm 139:14 NLT). We won't be body-shamed if we remember that God lovingly created us!

• •

Yes, Lord, You created me with beauty and perfection! Help me to walk in the truth that I am worthy!

67

Who's Keeping Tabs?

*The Lord appointed seventy-two others and
sent them two by two ahead of him to every
town and place where he was about to go.*
LUKE 10:1 NIV

Many of us moms seem to be hardwired to take care of our own business and make sure everyone else takes care of theirs. We spend years perfecting the art of tracking details and ensuring that our family stays on task. That "keeping tabs on everything" mentality might be a big part of the mom job description in our minds, but that doesn't mean it's how God wants us to be.

At times we get so accustomed to being the go-to person that it can be hard to realize we might not need to be the person keeping everything on an even keel. It's actually all right to step back and let the people around us handle some of those things themselves.

Jesus was the perfect example of how we should share accountability. Although Jesus was capable of doing anything that needed to be done, the Bible tells of several times when He gave instructions to His followers and expected them to handle the jobs. For example, Jesus asked Philip for suggestions on how to feed a crowd of thousands (John 6:5–7). Jesus

instructed two disciples to find a young donkey that He could ride into the city of Jerusalem (Mark 11:1–3). In some of His final directions, Jesus asked Peter and John to prepare a room where they could celebrate the Passover together (Luke 22:7–13). Jesus knew everything that needed to be done, but He didn't insist on doing everything Himself.

This loss of personal control can seem unsettling. But if we ask, God will show us what things others can do and what we should handle ourselves. After all, He's the ultimate master at keeping tabs on things.

• •

Lord, sometimes I'm afraid that if I don't keep up with everything going on with my family, no one will. But I know it shouldn't always be that way. Teach me to be like Jesus and ask others to step up and be responsible. Amen.

The Sweetest Alarm

In the morning You hear my voice, O Lord; in the
morning I prepare [a prayer, a sacrifice] for You and
watch and wait [for You to speak to my heart].
PSALM 5:3 AMPC

Until our children are ready to wake up on their own, we moms often play the role of alarm clock. It's a simple task but one that can provide some of the most precious moments of our day. For each mom and child it's different, but we might trace the slope of their noses or brush the hair out of their faces so that we can plant a soft kiss on their foreheads. Our whispered "Good morning" or "I love you" are the first words they hear.

God does the same for us. He caresses our faces with the warmth of fresh sunshine and makes us smile at the birds' morning chatter and songs. He whispers that He loves us and that He has great plans for us to follow. He reminds us that we don't have to face the day alone.

The problem is, answering a squawking alarm clock and focusing on morning routines can steal our attention from God's gentle wake-up call. We jump from bed and rush to get out the door. We think ahead to things that will need our attention that day in an attempt to stay one step ahead of the game. It might

seem counterproductive at first, but the best way we'll stay ahead is by stepping back. Even responding to God's wake-up call with a simple "Hello" or "Come be with me today" can put us in the right frame of mind for the day.

God delights in those early morning wake-up calls. We know how our children's drowsy smiles and hugs warm our hearts when we wake them. Taking a few minutes to tell God "Good morning" is just as pleasing to Him.

• •

Dear God, thank You for waking me to each new day. Remind me of Your presence, and show me ways to remember You're near, from the very minute I open my eyes. Amen.

Moms in Prayer

Lift up your hands to Him for the lives of your children.
LAMENTATIONS 2:19 HCSB

A group of moms joined the local Moms in Prayer group, committing themselves to pray for their kids while they were in junior high school. They saw the impact of their prayers, so they decided to keep praying for their children through high school, then through college. Although their kids are now adults, the moms still gather online. . .because they can't stop praying! It's true that a praying mother, who constantly intercedes and advocates for her children, is powerful.

We often hastily mumble words of prayer, especially when we are in a time crunch and the day seems to be getting out of hand. Sometimes we utter generic prayers without mention of anyone's name. But how quickly our prayers change when our children go through difficulties! . . . When a mom can't be with her son when he gets sick because they are on different continents. . . When another hasn't heard from an estranged daughter for years. . . Even when a mom requests a passing grade for that all-important subject. . . Every prayer makes the priority list when we are helpless and can't do much!

God never tires of hearing from us. He longs to connect with and answer us. We read in the book of Lamentations, "The hearts of the people cry out to the Lord. . . . Let your tears run down like a river day and night. Give yourself no relief and your eyes no rest. Arise, cry out in the night from the first watch of the night. Pour out your heart like water before the Lord's presence. Lift up your hands to Him for the lives of your children" (2:18–19 HCSB).

Did those verses strike a chord in your heart to become a mom in prayer? Do you feel the tug of commitment to start cultivating a heart of prayer for your children, covering them from here on until your last goodbye? Remember that a meaningful prayer to accompany your children will bless them tremendously!

• •

O God who hears and answers prayer,
I thank You that I can lift up my children
to You and ask You to be their guide!

Apple of His Eye

Keep me as the apple of your eye;
hide me in the shadow of your wings.
PSALM 17:8 NIV

It's not uncommon to hear that someone is the apple of another person's eye. We might have even said it about our own children, meaning that they're special to us and we love them in a way no one else can.

The phrase "apple of your eye" is found several times in the Bible, including one that literally translates as "the daughter of the eye" and means that one person is reflected in the eye of another. That's pretty amazing when we stop to think about it.

King David knew how much God loved him and how far God would go to protect him. When David asked God to keep him as the apple of His eye, he was asking God to see him as someone precious who needed to be protected.

Doesn't that sound like us with our children? We want to protect them whenever possible because they're precious to us. How amazing that God sees us in the same way! No matter who we are or how old we might be, God has a place in His heart especially for us.

We are the apple of God's eye just as our children hold that

place in ours—someone precious who He wants to protect. We need to remember that today but also remember what "apple of your eye" can mean from the other viewpoint—that we want God to see Himself reflected in us. Some days it can be hard to meet that standard, but God will help us take little steps toward it if we only ask.

Whether we need extra care and protection or just want to be more like God, we can face the day knowing that God delights in us. We're the apple of His eye!

• •

Dear God, thank You for loving me so much that I'm the apple of Your eye and someone who is precious to You. Help me to always remember that, and help me to grow in my faith so that You see Yourself in me. Amen.

Nudge to Something New

If any of you lacks wisdom, let him ask God, who gives generously to all without reproach, and it will be given him.
JAMES 1:5 ESV

All children have times when they're nervous—or maybe even downright scared—about trying something new. We can relate because we've been in that same spot ourselves.

As often as we might tell our children that stepping into unfamiliar territory can have real benefits and that they don't need to be worried, we don't always listen to our own assurances. It's often true that we are more tuned in to opportunities for our children than for ourselves. No wonder it can come as a surprise that God might have some new things waiting for us if we'll just pay attention.

We're never too old for new goals or new dreams, whether we set them for ourselves or God does it for us. God can certainly send us in some new directions or invite us to try some new things, even well into our adulthood—even when we're caught up in the world of motherhood.

The signs can be subtle, such as a long-buried interest or curiosity cropping up unexpectedly. Or we see or hear something that intrigues us but seems almost silly because it's so

different from our normal activities. A friend might introduce us to an activity we've never thought about before. When these things happen, they aren't always coincidences. Instead, they may be God telling us it's time to try something new. Before we rush on by, we need to take the advice we give our children: step back and focus on what we're feeling and where God might be leading us.

Just as we pray for wisdom when guiding our children, we need to ask for God's direction when we're trying to figure things out for ourselves. It's easy to get stuck in a rut and resist trying new things. But we need to remember that those new things make us better people and therefore better moms. Let's ask God to help us shake off the fear of unfamiliar territory.

• •

Dear Lord, I want my children to have courage and try new things, and I want the same for myself. Please don't let my routines block a path You might want me to follow. Give me the wisdom I need to know when You're calling me to something new. Amen.

A Mother's Tears

Weeping may last through the night,
but joy comes with the morning.
PSALM 30:5 NLT

Do you know how much weight a mother's tears carry, especially when she is praying? It speaks of her selfless love and sacrifice. It shows the depth of her emotions. And sometimes her prayer journal has proof of her dried tears marking its pages.

Shedding tears may be uncomfortable for some, but it helps open our bodies to release stress, sadness, grief, anxiety, and frustration. This detoxification process allows us to express the depth of our emotions as we seek to find healing. When we are in deep despair, we often mix prayers with our tears. Our sorrowful tears beg God to intervene in the pain we are feeling, to mercifully take it away from us. And if at times we find it difficult to put into words exactly how we feel, our tears still draw us to God in lament.

In Psalm 56:8 (NLT), David provided a beautiful picture of what God did for him in those sorrowful moments. He said, "You keep track of all my sorrows. You have collected all my tears in your bottle. You have recorded each one in your book."

Can you believe how aware God is of every single sorrow

we experience and every tear we cry, even recording them for remembrance? In our painful moments, we should remember that God's presence is with us, for He does not dismiss us and leave us to struggle alone. Instead, He wants to give us His tender comfort and assurance that He understands and loves us very much.

Although "weeping may last through the night," we know that the morning will end our weeping. Our joyful tears will finally come as God answers us with His strength and renewal. He will wipe away our sorrowful tears and remove our "clothes of mourning" (Psalm 30:11 NLT), so we can "sing praises to [Him] and not be silent" (v. 12 NLT) about the assurance that He will never leave us in our sorrow.

• •

We are blessed, dear heavenly Father, that You walk with us in our deepest pain and provide healing for it.

Mom Time

Very early the next morning before daylight, Jesus got up and went to a place where he could be alone and pray.
MARK 1:35 CEV

Diamonds may be a girl's best friend, as the old saying goes, but time to ourselves can be a mom's most precious gift. That's because mothering is a never-ending job, whether we're looking after little ones at home or keeping in touch with older kids in college or on their own.

Carving out time for ourselves so that we can unplug from being Mom for a while can be a challenge. But resisting the urge to feel guilty about giving that gift to ourselves can be the biggest hurdle of all. When the "I shouldn't be spoiling myself" or "I have too much to do" messages start crowding our minds, we should remember two important things. First, allowing ourselves some time alone is good for everyone in the family because we'll return to our mom world more refreshed and ready to handle things better. Second, even Jesus sometimes went away to be alone or to pray.

If Jesus had days when He needed to get away from the crowds, then why do we think it's a luxury we shouldn't indulge in? If we're honest, we'll see that the time away isn't a luxury

at all; it's a necessity. We need the chance to do things we enjoy instead of what everyone else needs (or expects) us to do. We need one-on-one time with God away from the normal routine to reconnect on a spiritual level by talking to Him and listening to Him.

It might be for an hour, half a day, or a weekend. The length of time doesn't matter as much as the fact that we're allowing ourselves to enjoy the gift. Because nothing will recharge our mom batteries like a mom-God getaway.

• •

Dear Lord, I need a break from family, from friends, from everyone and everything but You. Show me how to arrange things so that I can have a mom getaway, just You and me. Amen.

Doling Out Discipline

The LORD disciplines the one He loves,
just as a father, the son he delights in.
PROVERBS 3:12 HCSB

Our children are born with sweet dispositions, innocent minds, and pure hearts. We'd like to keep them that way, but sooner or later their humanness begins to show and they disobey us. Some missteps can be overlooked; others can be addressed with a simple conversation and time-out. Then we're faced with situations that call for serious discipline.

Punishing our children can be one of the toughest responsibilities of motherhood. We want to wrap them in a hug, get their promise that they won't do it again, and move on with assurance. When we look past our mother's hearts, however, we realize that approach isn't always what our children need.

The best way for our children to learn discipline is from us at home. Not that they'll necessarily understand our reasoning. We can probably cringe at remembering a time when our children threw the "You don't love me" accusation our way. The words cut straight through our hearts, but that's when we remind our children (and ourselves) that discipline comes from God and is part of our job as parents.

Several places in the Bible direct parents to discipline their children and teach that although it isn't fun at the moment, the benefits show in the long run. Verses also teach that we learn from being disciplined. Most importantly, we learn that disciplining our children is a way to show our love for them and that God also disciplines those He loves (see Proverbs 3:11–12).

Disciplining our children can be easier if we're prepared mentally and spiritually. We can start praying now that God will give us wisdom and our children understanding whenever that "next time" comes. Then we'll both grow from the experience and learn to honor God through it.

• •

Lord, disciplining my children can be so hard, but I know it needs to be done. Teach me to correct them while still showing love. Help them learn from it and understand my love for them will never change. Amen.

A Hard Decision to Make

"Never! Can a mother forget her nursing child?
Can she feel no love for the child she has borne?"
Isaiah 49:15 NLT

Laila was a young foreign student when she found herself pregnant. She chose to carry her baby while finishing her studies but gave her up for adoption. More than two decades later, she finally met her beautiful daughter and established a relationship with her and her adoptive parents.

Jochebed gave birth to a son at a time when Pharaoh gave strict instructions to the midwives to kill every son born to the Israelites. Fearing God, the midwives didn't obey Pharaoh but let the boys live. When Jochebed could no longer hide Moses, "she got a basket made of papyrus reeds and waterproofed it with tar and pitch. She put the baby in the basket and laid it among the reeds along the bank of the Nile River. The baby's sister then stood at a distance, watching to see what would happen to him" (Exodus 2:3–4 NLT). Pharaoh's daughter came to bathe in the river, and baby Moses was adopted as her own. By God's will, "[Jochebed] took her baby home and nursed him" (v. 9 NLT), caring for Moses as the hired nanny.

There are hard decisions that a mother sometimes makes;

and one such decision is putting a child up for adoption. The desire to do what's right for the child and to provide the child with a chance to thrive becomes the mother's priority. For Laila, it was an unplanned pregnancy and her inability to raise her daughter. For Jochebed, it was to save her son from death because of the edict.

Adoption is said to be a selfless decision, with each mother having a unique reason for giving up her child. Both Laila and Jochebed were blessed to have been part of their children's lives—Laila in her daughter's adult years; Jochebed in her son's growing years.

For adoptive moms—what a noble thing to forever change someone's life by providing a safe and loving home! You need to be celebrated as you open not only the doors of your homes but also your generous hearts in blessing someone.

• •

Thank You, Father, for being the ultimate parent to all of us! Teach us to lovingly nurture our children, biological or adopted.

DAY 40

Individual Love

The word of the LORD came to me, saying,
"Before I formed you in the womb I knew you,
before you were born I set you apart."
JEREMIAH 1:4–5 NIV

When our first child is born, we are often unprepared for the amount of love we feel. If we become pregnant with other children later, we might find it hard to believe that we can love any other child as much as our oldest. But then the new baby arrives, and we learn that all the assurances from well-meaning parents were true: we have more than enough love to spread around. In some sort of heart-based multiplication that only God could plan, we're able to love each child in abundance and as an individual. We never need to take love away from one child to have enough for the other.

The same concept is true for our relationship with God. No matter how many children are born or how many of us follow God, He has more than enough love for everyone and loves us equally and as unique individuals.

God doesn't care whether our figure is curvy or straight, and doesn't prefer blonds or brunettes over redheads. He doesn't think people with noticeable talents are more important than

those of us who prefer to stay in the background. And although billions of people populate this earth, God never loses us in the crowd. He sees us and loves every detail that makes us unique, from the whorl of our fingerprints to each gray hair we might try to hide. We're unique and special because God made us to be that way. Nothing we do—or don't do—will ever make Him love us more or less than anyone else.

What a reason to celebrate ourselves and God's love! It's time to thank God for making us each a one-of-a-kind woman and mom—and for doing the same for each of our children.

• •

Thank You, God, for making me who I am.
Help me to learn to appreciate my uniqueness
and remember that You love me just as I am...
and just as much as anyone else. Amen.

Who's Really Listening?

"Listen to my prayer and my plea, O Lord my God. Hear the cry and the prayer that your servant is making to you."
2 Chronicles 6:19 nlt

Some days, it feels like no matter what we say or who we say it to, no one hears us. Our husband and children are caught up in a favorite television show or have their earbuds locked in place. The boss is focused on sales figures or is anxious about meeting with a prospective client. Our friend is too wrapped up in planning her daughter's wedding to notice much else. It makes us grateful that we can hear ourselves speaking so that we know at least one person is listening. Even if it's just us.

Those days can be drive-us-crazy frustrating, but what if we look at it a different way? We're guaranteed to have at least one listener other than ourselves whenever we speak, and He's the best listener of all. God never slumbers or sleeps (see Psalm 121:3), which means He's always there when we're ready to talk. He hears each prayer about whatever's on our minds (see Psalm 66:19). Whether we're talking through options as we try to reach a decision or muttering to ourselves about our shopping list, we're talking—and God is listening.

The next time a "no one's listening to me" day rolls around, it

can be a chance to remind ourselves that God is always listening, no matter the day or time or what we're trying to tell someone. It might even be a good idea to walk away from everyone else and start our conversation with God by venting about our day or how we're feeling ignored. Once that frustration is off our minds, we can say whatever we tried to tell the people around us. And then, we listen. Because we never know what God might have to share with us when it's His turn to talk.

• •

Thank You, Lord, for always listening to me whenever I'm ready to talk, even when no one else seems to pay any attention. Help me to turn those days into special times to communicate with You. Amen.

Be Careful How We Live

Post this at all the intersections, dear friends:
Lead with your ears, follow up with your tongue,
and let anger straggle along in the rear. God's
righteousness doesn't grow from human anger.
JAMES 1:19–20 MSG

"I remember an incident as a child when you were so mad at me because you thought I lost our dinner coupon. When you finally found it in your purse, your anger was just gone. . .as if nothing happened. Where was your apology to me?" an adult daughter said to her mother. Surprised, the mother blurted, "I am sorry that happened. I don't even remember that day, as it's been a long time ago." The downside to this story is that the child, a mother today, sees the same anger building up in herself.

Anger is instinctive. When we feel frustrated, threatened, or attacked, our emotions get stirred and we get angry. In the heat of the moment, we often allow anger to overtake us instead of calming ourselves down. Anger becomes almost like a weapon we brandish, making us attack first before we get attacked.

James said to "let anger straggle along in the rear." *Straggle* is a very interesting verb to use with anger in a sentence.

Imagine a turtle as the picture word for *straggle*, moving ever so slowly that you don't know if it will ever reach the finish line. Let anger trail far behind so that it doesn't catch up with you. In this way, anger can fall by the wayside and there will be no need to react negatively.

James followed up with "God's righteousness doesn't grow from human anger." If we hold on to self-preservation and self-righteousness, it will be hard for us to allow God to work out His righteousness in us. In our anger, we forget about the love that God tells us should govern us so that we can "let anger straggle along in the rear" and not be led to hurt others.

Our children are watching how we live, and our anger can get in the way of showing what God's love and goodness are all about. In our anger, we dishonor God. We need to lose anger—and lose it quick!

• •

Lord, forgive me for the anger that I allow to control my emotions. Take hold of it!

A True Reflection

So our faces are not covered. They show the bright
glory of the Lord, as the Lord's Spirit makes us
more and more like our glorious Lord.
2 CORINTHIANS 3:18 CEV

Before our children are born, we enjoy imagining how they'll look. And later, people seem to enjoy sharing whether they think the children favor us or our husband or are a good blend of both. The truth is, though, that our children's appearances change as they grow.

The same should be true of our inward appearances—they should change because of our relationship with God. As humans, we're all made in God's image (see Genesis 1:27). As Christians, we're meant to be a reflection of God through our thoughts, actions, and beliefs. We won't ever be a perfect reflection of God because we make mistakes. Sin tempts us and sometimes traps us just like anyone else. But every time we back up from the wrong place, ask for forgiveness (from God and anyone else involved in the situation), and try again, the image of God within us shines through a little brighter.

Our children see God in us when we apologize for short-comings, respect their opinions, or pray with them. Strangers

see God in us when we hold our tempers instead of reacting in frustration when our children annoy us in public. Other parents see God in us when we share each other's burdens and support each other through difficult times.

We don't need to try so hard to show God in our lives that we nearly blind people with our efforts. Day-to-day authentic attempts to follow God will reflect Him in just the right ways so that others will be drawn to us (and God) over time instead of driven away. Let's honor our heavenly Father by challenging ourselves to reflect God to others each time we see them.

• •

Dear Lord, I love You and want others to learn about You through what they see in me. Show me how I can be a true reflection of You in every situation. Amen.

Praying for Prodigals

"While he was still a long way off, his father saw him and was filled with compassion for him; he ran to his son, threw his arms around him and kissed him."
Luke 15:20 niv

Lauren is in a position she never imagined would be possible: she is the mom of a prodigal child. Her daughter graduated from high school, moved out of state to find a job, and never contacted her family again. There was no big fight, no struggle with rebellion, no reason given for the change. Her daughter simply moved on with her life and out of theirs.

Repeated searches to find her have failed. Attempted communications through people who might know where she is have been dead ends. All Lauren and her husband can do is pray. They continually ask God to protect their daughter and to remind her of their love. They hold on to the hope that she might have a change of heart and return to them one day.

Most of us will never know the extreme pain involved with having a prodigal child. Unfortunately, the same can't always be said for our relationship with God. Our closeness with God goes through different phases. At times, we find ourselves excited about everything connected with our faith. We plan

time to read the Bible and pray, we look forward to church each Sunday, we focus on following God's directions. Then, for whatever reason, we enter a not-so-close phase. Other things fill our days, and we drift away from God. If something extreme happens, we might consciously turn our backs on God and pretend He's not a part of our lives at all.

Whatever we may think or feel, God is never out of our lives. Just like Lauren and other parents of prodigals are eager to welcome their children back home, God will wait for us however long we're away. He always says "yes" when we want to come back to Him.

• •

Dear God, I can't imagine how hard it must be to have a prodigal child, yet I do the same thing to You more often than I'd like to admit. Forgive me for when I turn away. Thank You for always waiting for me. Amen.

Can We Really Spare Our Kids from Pain?

The LORD is close to the brokenhearted;
he rescues those whose spirits are crushed.
PSALM 34:18 NLT

After suffering through a season of frustration, a daughter confronted her mother and told her how unfair she was to keep her dying father's true condition from her. "I wanted to be there for Dad too, and you didn't give me a chance!" The mother explained that she was trying to protect her from the pain of losing her father while she was going through her divorce.

Can we really spare our children from pain without hurting them? We sometimes walk on eggshells, trying to shield our children from unpleasant circumstances. If we can sugarcoat the reality of loss and grief and make protecting our kids our purpose, perhaps the harsh truth will not be as painful. We can carry our burden along with theirs.

Proverbs 24:10 (NLT) says, "If you fail under pressure, your strength is too small." If this happens to our kids, it's because we robbed them of an important lesson. We didn't teach them how to be resilient in adversity. We didn't allow them to process

the situation in their own way so that they could get past it in their own time. How then can we expect our children to rise above unhappy news and cope with temporary setbacks?

In painful times, the best thing we can do is sit our children down. Depending on their ages, we'll share details that they can handle. The words of the apostle Paul explain it well: "What we suffer now is nothing compared to the glory he will reveal to us later. . . . And we know that God causes everything to work together for the good of those who love God and are called according to his purpose for them" (Romans 8:18, 28 NLT). Our faith in Christ should give us hope, so we need to impress the truth of God's Word on our kids!

We can't prevent suffering from happening. We can't prevent it from reaching our kids either. God calls us to teach our children His Word. We need to trust Him for ourselves and for our children.

• •

Thank You, Lord, for walking with me
and my children in every circumstance!
Help me to trust You always.

Best Gifts of All

*God sent his Son into the world not to judge
the world, but to save the world through him.*
JOHN 3:17 NLT

Few things make us happier as a parent than being able to give something to our children that we know they'll love. Whatever sacrifices we make to reach that point are worth it when we see their surprise and joy. God has gifts for us all the time, but they're not reserved for our birthday, Christmas, or another special occasion. Some gifts are so small that we might not notice them every day, like a bird's song or wildflowers along the road. Others are so big that we can't ignore them, like being spared from a hurricane or tornado's path or having a perfect but unexpected opportunity fall in our laps.

The biggest and best gift God has given us is through His Son, Jesus. God sent Jesus to live on earth so that people could learn about Him and want to follow Him. The culmination of God's plan was for Jesus to die on the cross in our place so that we can spend eternity in heaven with God instead of being separated forever.

Sending Jesus to earth wasn't an easy thing for God to do, and watching Jesus die on the cross was the worst part of all.

We cannot even imagine going through that as a parent. But God did it because of what it would mean in the long run: righteous sons and daughters for eternity. The joy we would have at being invited to live forever in heaven mirrored God's pleasure at giving it to us and made everything worthwhile.

We know how much it warms our hearts to hear a sincere "thank you" from our children when we give them a special gift. Why don't we do the same for God today?

• •

Dear Lord, thank You so much for giving me the best gift of all-knowledge of Your Son, Jesus, and the chance to spend eternity with You in heaven. Help me to never take it for granted! Amen.

Time to Feast

Jesus said to them, "I am the bread of life;
whoever comes to me shall not hunger,
and whoever believes in me shall never thirst."
JOHN 6:35 ESV

It's one of the age-old questions posed to moms around the world: what's for dinner? Whether we're celebrating with steak and lobster or scraping by with hot dogs or PB&J until the next paycheck, the menus all have something in common. The food staves off hunger and, hopefully, nourishes and strengthens our bodies.

What we put on their plates might please our children or disappoint. Regardless, they trust us to think ahead of their needs and give them what we think is best. That's why it's important to ask ourselves: Are we filling their spiritual hunger on a regular basis as well? And how are we keeping ourselves filled?

Finding time to renew ourselves spiritually can be difficult. But just like our bodies can't survive indefinitely without food and drink, our spiritual selves will wither and fade without regular nourishment. The signs of spiritual malnourishment crop up quickly. Anxiety fills our minds. Surly words pop from our mouths. Negative thoughts control our attitudes.

Fortunately, the cure for a hungry soul is always within reach. Sometimes it's best approached in small steps, just like a person who hasn't eaten for a long time starts with only a few bites of food. We can take five minutes to read a short devotional, or we can listen to Christian music while we run errands or exercise. We can choose a Bible verse to memorize each week or start a list of ways we notice God around us.

Each little thing will build on the others until we've re-established a two-way connection with God. As long as we keep that foundation in place, our souls will be satisfied. Then we can take what we've learned and teach it to our children so that they'll also be filled.

● ●

Lord, I usually rush to satisfy my physical hunger at the first rumbling of my stomach. Help me to pay just as much attention to my spiritual hunger so that I can fill myself with what matters most: You. Amen.

Messages of Love

Let love and faithfulness never leave you.
PROVERBS 3:3 NIV

She worried for her young son, who was barely out of high school and now on deployment. To alleviate her own fears and worries, she decided to record a daily three-hour audio message on a cassette tape. She talked about her day and her best wishes for her son. She prayed as well. And each day for one year, she traveled five miles to the nearest post office to send off her message of love.

Encouraged by his mom's loving dedication, the son did the same. While he was on regular night duty aboard the naval vessel somewhere in the Gulf, he recorded how his day went and what he saw while on guard.

Imagine the impact of that one-year exchange of messages of love between a mother and her son! The daily commitment alone would overwhelm many today. Try sending a text message to your son or daughter, and you might get a response a few hours or days later or maybe no response. Or you might even be reprimanded with a "You don't need to check up on me!" message.

In the Old Testament, Moses summoned Joshua, his

successor, to prepare him to lead Israel. Moses would no longer be around, so he encouraged Joshua with these words: "The LORD himself goes before you and will be with you; he will never leave you nor forsake you. Do not be afraid; do not be discouraged" (Deuteronomy 31:8 NIV). Moses' message of love provided Joshua with a God-focused encouragement. It wasn't about how great Joshua was but about how God will deliver.

In the same manner, the wisdom of Proverbs says, "Let love and faithfulness never leave you; bind them around your neck, write them on the tablet of your heart" (3:3 NIV). God is love and faithfulness personified. He is telling us to write His message of love in our hearts and to display His faithfulness for all to see. If we cling to Him, especially in times of fear and worry, He will go before us and be our encouragement.

• •

Gracious Father, thank You that You are love and faithfulness and that we can trust You with all our heart!

Mama Bear

*The Lord will rescue me from every evil attack and
will bring me safely to his heavenly kingdom.*
2 TIMOTHY 4:18 NIV

We've heard the analogies, seen the cartoons, or even fulfilled
the role ourselves: Mama Bear, doing whatever is needed to
protect her young, no matter the cost. That protective instinct
might lie dormant and unnoticed for much of our lives. Then
we become a mom, and it's as if something inside us shifts. We
know without a doubt that we'll do anything in the world for our
child. No questions asked, no excuses given. How reassuring
to know that God feels the same way about us.

Many stories in the Bible tell us how God protected those
who loved and followed Him. God kept the Israelites safe in the
desert for forty years until they reached their new homeland.
He protected armies and gave them victory over more powerful opponents multiple times. God told people how to ensure
their safety when their enemies or oppressors were bent on
destroying them.

The ways God protects us today might not seem so obvious
or far-reaching, but that doesn't make them less important.
We'll never know how many traffic accidents God has saved

us from or how much damage was avoided when a hurricane dissipates while still far off shore. We lock our doors at night, having no idea how many thieves God steers away from our homes.

Bad things will still happen because we live in a world full of sin. Even in bad times, though, we can thank God for teaching us through those experiences and for protecting us from worse things. We stand ready to protect our children throughout their lives, no matter how old they get. How good to know that God stands as our perfect example and gives us the courage to be Mama Bear when needed.

• •

Dear God, thank You for loving and protecting me in all the ways I know about, but especially for the unseen ways. I praise You for being my faithful protector. Amen.

Days into Years

*A thousand years in your sight are like a day that
has just gone by, or like a watch in the night.*
PSALM 90:4 NIV

Round-the-clock baby routines begin as soon as we bring
our children home from the hospital, and the calendar starts
playing tricks on us. Some days creep by so slowly that we feel
like we'll be stuck in the phase of constant diapers and near-
constant sleep deprivation forever. But time continues to slip
past, and before we realize what's happening, we're planning
a first birthday party. Then in what seems like no time at all,
we're registering them for kindergarten. . .and middle school
. . .and beyond. We live in a strange mix of some days going
slowly and others racing by.

We lock time into specific increments to help us keep
track of our lives—seconds, minutes, hours, days. But God
has no need for those constraints because He's always present, everywhere, all the time. Before our children are born,
God sees them on their wedding day and with babies of their
own. God knows their chosen profession, their best friend,
and everything they'll experience. We can barely wrap our
minds around God being here throughout all time, but we

don't have to understand it to appreciate it. We just need to trust that He was with us in the past, is with us today, and will be with us in the future.

On those days when we feel like we're living in some kind of time warp, we should remember that we weren't really made to be boxed in by time. God created us with hearts set on eternity (Ecclesiastes 3:11). That means our bodies might be here, but our souls are ready to spend eternity with God. Think about it: God doesn't care about our clocks. God cares about eternity—and He already has plans to spend it with us!

• •

Dear Lord, I don't understand how time moves by or how You're present in all of it. But I'm glad that You are and that You're always watching over my children and me. Thank You for waiting for me to join You in eternity. Amen.

Now Is Not Forever

Behold, children are a heritage from the
LORD, the fruit of the womb a reward.
PSALM 127:3 ESV

An expectant mom excitedly selects items using the store's handheld scanner or picks and chooses online what to register for her baby. She hops from one fun baby shower to another and accumulates all the cute baby items on her list. She agonizes over design ideas as she prepares the nursery. But the minute she gives birth and the 24-7 reality of nurturing the newborn hits, she sometimes wishes she could be at a different place on the timeline.

Now is not forever!—the opposite of a new mom's dilemma. Worn out by sleepless nights and less self-care, she imagines life will always be this way. No matter how organized she tries to be, that catnap sounds better than dealing with the laundry that needs to be washed or the dirty plates that are piling up in the kitchen sink.

But there are also those who have easily bounced back and already found the right groove. They are able to enjoy moments of perfectly posed mother-and-child photos with cute announcements and thoughtful messages on stylized sandwich boards.

Motherhood is one of the best and biggest learning experiences in our life. We can read as many books about it as we want. We can spend time researching online. But our hands-on experience will reveal timeless truths that a manual or article cannot contain. We just live it!

The book of Psalms says, "Behold, children are a heritage from the LORD, the fruit of the womb a reward." Imagine the beauty of creation we have been part of. . .that came out of our bodies. What an honor to be God's vessels!

Life has seasons, and motherhood is one of them. Establishing that special bond through unconditional love is very powerful. Just as we were when we were expecting, let's be as excited now with the relationship we can create together. There are many beautiful memories to make so that we can look back with love at the million ways we shared moments together.

• • • • • • • • • • • • • • • • • •

What a blessing to be a mother! Help me, Lord, to remember this so that I can enjoy motherhood.

All Wrapped Up

O LORD, I am your servant....
You have loosed my bonds.
PSALM 116:16 ESV

What is it about tape—Scotch tape, masking tape, duct tape—that's so fascinating to children? They use it to hold the world together, create purses or wallets, label their possessions, and make balls that reach grapefruit size. Sometimes they pretend the tape is a bandage and wrap it around their fingers or toes. That's usually when we moms get pulled into the situation because too many layers of tape can restrict blood flow. If we're lucky, the tape peels off in long strips that are easy to manage instead of little bits that frustrate our child and make them feel like they're not making progress.

Sounds like situations we get ourselves into, doesn't it? We've all been bound at some point, whether it's in a relationship we should end or a behavior we should break or a change we're scared to make. It can be far too easy for us to get stuck that way—and extremely difficult to break free.

Just like our children with the tape, we might try to set ourselves free. Sometimes it works, but many times we fail. We simply weren't meant to handle things alone. God can give

us encouragers to love and support us as we move in a new direction. We just need to set aside our independence and pride and ask for the help we need.

When we're trapped in a situation or think our children might be, God will show us what to do and when to do it. Our first step is to ask God for wisdom and take time to listen for the answer. When we follow God's direction, He can free us from any situation or show us how we can be the help that someone else needs.

• •

Lord, give me wisdom to avoid places where I don't need to be. Thank You for saving me when I get into those tight spots and want a way out. Thank You for being the only one who can truly free me. Amen.

House Clutter and Heart Clutter

Create in me a pure heart, O God,
and renew a steadfast spirit within me.
PSALM 51:10 NIV

Our definition of *cluttered* can vary a lot from our children's, particularly when they're young. They see piles of plastic bricks waiting to be built into castles; we see a Lego explosion. They see some clothes on the floor; we see an avalanche of laundry that could bury a small child. Then there are all the things stashed under beds, shoved behind bureaus, and crammed into closets that our children don't mind and we're not supposed to notice.

House clutter can be easy to see and fairly easy to tidy. Heart clutter, on the other hand, is much more difficult to see, and cleaning it up can be complicated, hard work. Let's face it: it takes courage to start digging into the corners of our hearts and minds, uncovering old hurts, jealousies, or insecurities buried just beneath the surface. Anger, pride, or fear can be lurking in the shadows. We keep thinking that we can leave it there and God won't notice.

Just as our kids don't fool us for long with their shove-everything-away tactics, we won't be able to hide the clutter in our hearts from God. He sees everything. We have to drag each piece into the light so that we can acknowledge it, deal with it, and move on. At least we don't have to make the journey alone. God already knows what's in our hearts, so nothing we pull out will surprise Him. We can rely on God to give us the strength to face whatever is there. It will take time, and it won't always be easy. But the end result will be worth every struggle: a heart that is freshly de-cluttered and focused on God.

• •

Dear Lord, it's so much easier to see the clutter and junk around me than what's buried in my heart. Give me the courage to dig in there and find what needs to be changed. Thank You for helping me do it. Amen.

Starting Over

*"Look, I am about to do something new;
even now it is coming."*
ISAIAH 43:19 HCSB

Do you know what the problem is with starting over? It is the end of things as well! And the starting over and ending of things can mean lots of things—from getting married to becoming a new mom to becoming an empty nester. It may mean giving up a career to raise kids full-time. Or it may be the loss of a husband down the road, making us widows. Some of the seasons will bring excitement and joy, while others will bring loss and grief.

Israel had a lot of starting-overs to do. For hundreds of years, the Israelites were Egyptian slaves until called out to be God's people and the great exodus happened. But on their way to the Promised Land, they had to wander in the wilderness for forty years. God had to strip them and show them how to start over and embrace their new identity. He gave them commandments and statutes to remind them how to live.

Reaching their inheritance and settling in the land, the Israelites had many rough and tough moments. They forgot to live obediently and found themselves living in defeat and

captivity. In the book of Isaiah, God reminded them of their idolatrous behavior and told them what He would do so that they could start over. He said, "Do not fear, for I am with you; I will bring your descendants from the east, and gather you from the west.... Bring My sons from far away, and My daughters from the ends of the earth. . . . Look, I am about to do something new; even now it is coming" (43:5–6, 19 HCSB).

Are you on the threshold of starting over? Perhaps you are afraid to step into the new chapter because you doubt your ability. Don't fear! Think of new discoveries you will have about yourself.

And God wants to be part of this too! Remember that God wants to do a brand-new thing. . .and, surprisingly, it has already started!

• •

Lord, I know that starting over is part of life.
I ask for Your wisdom and encouragement
as I step into new beginnings!

Interruptions Welcome

*If our hearts condemn us, we know that God is
greater than our hearts, and he knows everything.*
1 JOHN 3:20 NIV

We've all had them: days when it seems like we're being interrupted more often than not. We just get settled into doing something—then the phone, the email, the pet, the children . . .knock us off track again. It can be enough to drive us crazy.

The first few times it happens, we might be able to take a deep breath, smile, and not be too bothered. Our smile and patience can be harder to keep in place as the interruptions mount. We might even reach the point of telling our children to only interrupt us again if someone is sick, bleeding, or has a broken bone.

Sometimes we fall into the pattern of approaching God the same way. If a problem or request isn't life-shattering, we think it's not worth praying about. We rationalize by saying God has more important things to deal with. God does have things on His "watch list" that we don't know about and can't understand. The best news is, God can also tune into all the small things of everyday life without losing His grip on the big things.

Nothing will ever bump us off God's radar. Nothing we pray

about is seen as an interruption, however insignificant it might seem in comparison to other issues. After all, God is all about the details and the little things. We only have to look at the intricate, interwoven pieces of creation to understand that. The same concept still applies when we look at our own lives.

What a joy it is when we realize we can bring everything to God, from the biggest dilemma to the smallest question or irritation. It's never an interruption. And the freedom of opening up could draw us closer to God than we expect.

Dear God, my problems usually aren't very important compared to everything else in the world. But You still love me and want to hear from me, no matter what's on my mind. Thank You for never seeing me as an interruption. Amen.

Support Welcomed

*You and these people who come to you will only
wear yourselves out. The work is too heavy
for you; you cannot handle it alone.*
EXODUS 18:18 NIV

Years ago, commercials claimed that a woman who wore a certain brand of perfume could bring home the bacon, fry it up in a pan, and keep everyone in her family satisfied. Nothing was too much to handle for the modern woman. Wouldn't it be nice if life were that simple?

We're too smart to believe our perfume will help us get through our day any easier. But sometimes we can still fall into the trap of thinking we never need help. Worse yet, we can buy into the expectation that we're *supposed* to do everything for everyone because we're Mom. God gives us a big "no" to that line of thinking.

The Bible shares a prime example of a person who tried to do too much alone. When Moses led the Israelites out of Egypt toward their new land, he soon became exhausted from the responsibility of overseeing thousands of people. One of his most time-consuming jobs was hearing and passing judgment on disputes. His father-in-law saw what was happening and

suggested that Moses appoint other men to hear most of the disputes. Moses would only get involved with the complicated cases (see Exodus 18:13–26).

Although God called Moses to be the leader, he couldn't do it alone. He needed other, trusted helpers to handle certain things. Moses was capable but wasn't too proud to get help. The lesson for us is the same. God blessed us with being moms and expects us to do our best—but He doesn't always expect us to do everything ourselves. We are not the woman from the old perfume commercial. We are real-life women depending on God to help us be the best moms possible. Asking others to help worked for Moses. It can work for us too if we'll just ask.

• •

Dear God, I want to do everything possible for my family but know that realistically, I can't do it all. Give me the ability to ask for help and appreciate what's given. Amen.

119

A Lesson on Simplicity

Strength and dignity are her clothing.
PROVERBS 31:25 ESV

Marlene received a card from her daughter. The beautiful message touched her heart: "Thank you for passing on your words of wisdom that real beauty is not found in the exterior but on the inside."

Some women like to follow makeup trends, even teaching themselves how to apply cartoonish eyeliner and blush while batting very full eyelash extensions that make you wonder if they can still see clearly. It could also be fashion trends that are head-turners on runways for models but are an uncomfortable disaster as everyday wear. Yes, there is no denying that we would all look fabulous if we had our own glam squad and fashion stylists to prepare us every day!

In the Bible, Timothy said this about women: "I also want the women to dress modestly, with decency and propriety, adorning themselves, not with elaborate hairstyles or gold or pearls or expensive clothes, but with good deeds, appropriate for women who profess to worship God" (1 Timothy 2:9–10 NIV). The apostle Peter confirmed it: "Your beauty should not come from outward adornment, such as elaborate hairstyles and the

wearing of gold jewelry or fine clothes. Rather, it should be that of your inner self, the unfading beauty of a gentle and quiet spirit, which is of great worth in God's sight" (1 Peter 3:3–4 NIV).

This isn't about dressing in sackcloth and throwing ash on our heads like in mourning. It's discovering that simplicity is not flashy apparel and dolled-up faces to attract attention but our undeniable confidence in our inner beauty, which is anchored in our relationship with Jesus Christ. We cannot claim to be godly women if we don't live godly lives—and that includes how we present ourselves.

Both Timothy and Peter spoke of a great goal for followers of Christ: to live lives that are holy and pleasing to God. We are to focus not on attracting attention to our physical beauty but on displaying godliness with our quiet and gentle spirit.

• • • • • • • • • • • • • • • • • • • •

Lord, help me to focus on You and how
I can please and honor You!

Your Mother's Mouth

Set a guard, O LORD, over my mouth;
keep watch over the door of my lips!
PSALM 141:3 ESV

"I'll never say that to my children!" How many times did we think or say that when we were growing up? Certain things our mothers said incensed us and we promised to never utter those same words to our own children. Then we became moms and everything changed. We suddenly understood how frustrating the world of motherhood can be and that the challenges didn't disappear as our children grew older. Age just brought different frustrations.

When we're pushed too near our breaking point, it's not easy to control our emotions or our words. When we aren't sure how to handle a situation, the response we've heard before—the words from our own moms—might be the only one that comes to mind. Ultimatums, opinions, or less-than-stellar comments can pop out of our mouths before we can bite our tongues to stop them.

Words are a powerful force that can either encourage or defeat. Authors, philosophers, religious leaders, and others have expounded on the power of words for years. The Bible

also includes repeated advice about controlling our words and the potential aftereffects of careless speech. The tongue holds the power of life and death (Proverbs 18:21) and can either cut like a sword or bring healing (Proverbs 12:18). Ideally, the words we speak should build up other people and honor God (Psalm 19:14).

Because we can have so much trouble controlling our words, let's not tackle the problem alone. Let's confide in a trusted friend and ask for her prayers. Our friend might actually struggle with the same thing and ask us to pray for her too. Then we'll both be better equipped to speak words that are pleasing to God instead of resorting to ones we'd rather not say.

• •

Lord, I need help guarding my tongue
because I don't always do a very good job
controlling it on my own. Show me when to
speak and what to say so that I honor
You with all my words. Amen.

Bragging Rights

In God we make our boast all day long,
and we will praise your name forever.
PSALM 44:8 NIV

We have many reasons to be proud of our children, whatever their age. Good grades in school, being invited to join a select group, or landing a coveted job position can make us want to cash in on our bragging rights. We're sure other people would be interested in the accomplishment and want to congratulate our child. Spreading the word about something noteworthy isn't a bad thing, is it? The best answer is, "That depends."

Many Bible verses warn against bragging as a way to puff ourselves up or to show off in front of others. Some also tell of consequences for acting this way, such as not being rewarded by God. We don't want to fall into that trap just because we see or hear other moms tooting their children's horns. A few other Bible verses, however, teach when it can be acceptable to boast: when we're boasting about God and His work.

God gives each of us our intelligence, abilities, and other qualities that might lead to something brag-worthy. There's nothing wrong with sharing these special things, as long as we remember they're rooted in God and we teach our children

to do the same. Before emailing friends and family or posting something to our favorite social network, we should take a few minutes to thank God for helping our children succeed. We could even include our children in that prayer so that they could hear our thanks firsthand and also offer their own.

Once we've taken that step, we can ask God if it's appropriate to spread the news and, if so, to help us have a humble attitude when doing it. Then our child's situation will be a win/win/win from every perspective.

● ●

Thank You, Lord, for all the times You help my children accomplish things that we're proud of. Show me when it's appropriate to share those things outside our family, but help me not to cross the line from humble thankfulness to bragging. Amen.

How to Avoid Clutter in Your Life

"For where your treasure is, there your heart will be also."
MATTHEW 6:21 NIV

Have you ever walked through an estate sale? You find all sorts of castoffs ranging from art to clothes to household items. You see people browsing through the haphazard displays, assessing the items' values and making bargain offers to get them out of the hands of the sellers. Do you know what happens to the unsold items? They are either hauled away for donation or thrown in the dumpster.

Let's look around our homes and see what collectors we have turned into. We intentionally pick up clutter, thinking that our homes will look more comfortable and lived in if we have hundreds of photos hanging on the walls and memorabilia from our travels displayed on shelves and more. We believe in the memories held by these treasures, even using them as conversation pieces.

But Jesus said, "Do not store up for yourselves treasures on earth, where moths and vermin destroy, and where thieves break in and steal. But store up for yourselves treasures in

heaven, where moths and vermin do not destroy, and where thieves do not break in and steal. For where your treasure is, there your heart will be also" (Matthew 6:19–21 NIV).

Somehow, we are drawn to collecting clutter. Often, they are just things that have meaning to us. And it's hard to fight the urge to purchase when we are bombarded with messages to buy more and more.

But how would our homes look if we let go of our treasure-hunting desires and clutter collections? Will our homes look sterile if we don't layer with multiple light sources or mix and match textures and accessories? Are we going to miss the traffic jam caused by our furniture pieces scattered all over the house?

The sobering truth is we cannot bring our clutter with us when we pass. Nothing counts as real treasure in comparison to the eternal life Jesus offers. That only increases in immeasurable value as we live out our salvation until we reach our beautiful home in eternity.

• •

I ask, Lord, that You help me to think of eternity with You as my treasure!

Weeping for the World

Weeping may endure for a night,
but joy comes in the morning.
PSALM 30:5 AMPC

The world is full of things we'd rather not witness. Reports of natural disasters, poverty, human trafficking, war, and violence fill the local news each night. The stories disturb us, but we still listen because we believe "staying current" is important. Then we become mothers, and everything changes. Every event takes on new meaning when we filter it through mom eyes. Our hearts break for the women associated with those stories, the moms whose children are lost or injured or buried. We can feel a connection with these strangers not because we've experienced the same things personally but because we can barely fathom their grief or terror.

The moms on the news are broken, and so are we. That brokenness drives us to hug our children tighter, to thank God for them more sincerely. It leads us to wonder how we would handle the same situation ourselves.

The answer is given repeatedly in the Bible and has been shared countless times by pastors, teachers, and real-life friends. We get through seemingly unbearable situations

because God loves us and gives us the strength to keep moving from one moment to the next. We cling to the promise that each day gives us a fresh start. We comfort ourselves by remembering that God cries with us when tragedies occur. God is the one who mends our shattered hearts and gives us new hope, even if it only comes as the tiniest glimmer.

We'll never meet those women in the news, but that doesn't keep us from knowing them. The next time we hear a story that brings us to tears, let's take time to pray for the moms. Let's ask God to remind us—and them—that no matter how difficult today might be, joy comes in the morning.

• •

Dear Lord, some of the stories on the news leave me speechless and shocked. I don't know the moms involved, but You do. Give them peace. Show me how I can pray for them or if there are other things I can do to help. Amen.

Finding Our Worth

To all who did receive him, to those who believed in his
name, he gave the right to become children of God.
JOHN 1:12 NIV

Few things warm a mother's heart more than seeing her children's accomplishments. It's only human to want to do well in life and want the same for our children. We work hard to give them the opportunities they need to excel and to be prepared for adulthood. Somehow their success feels like a confirmation that all the patience and hard work we've invested was worth the effort. But what does a mother do when her children aren't quite as successful as she might have expected? Can she still be proud of her children and validated as a mother? We know the answer to that question should be an automatic and heartfelt "yes." But that's not always the way it happens. We moms don't always feel the way we know we should feel.

When it comes to achievements, there are two important lessons God wants us to learn and remember: First, the number of accomplishments we can add to our personal list of achievements doesn't define us as a person. Second, our children's accomplishments (or lack thereof) don't define us as moms. Failing to understand these two truths can bring regret and

condemnation to our lives and harm our relationships with our children.

Our true identity is found only in God. We are His daughters, princesses in His kingdom. Claiming that title as our own and believing what it means is more important than anything we can do, say, or try to plan for. Teaching our children that belonging to God is more valuable than any accolade they might ever receive is one of the most important gifts we can give them. Let's ask God to help us believe it ourselves so that we can pass it to our children.

• •

Thank You, God, for loving me enough to claim me as Your daughter. Help me to never forget that's the most important title or accomplishment I can ever have. Show me how to teach it to my children so that they know it themselves. Amen.

When Achievements Seem to Matter More

Yes, everything else is worthless when compared with the infinite value of knowing Christ Jesus my Lord.
PHILIPPIANS 3:8 NLT

Moms often like to regale friends and acquaintances with their children's academic accomplishments, sports victories, and stellar careers. But in their boasting, they seem to overlook some facts about their kids, such as the number of attempts to pass the bar or the reality that they are not living for the Lord. The only goal is to impress people and to hear the oohs and aahs.

The apostle Paul was such a highly credentialed person that he sounded boastful when he talked about it. He said, "I was a member of the Pharisees, who demand the strictest obedience to the Jewish law. I was so zealous that I harshly persecuted the church. And as for righteousness, I obeyed the law without fault" (Philippians 3:5–6 NLT). Paul had reached the highest ideal for a Jew to attain. He belonged to the elite of the religious, and he obeyed the laws and traditions exactly as they were laid out.

But Paul's encounter with Jesus on the road to Damascus

took him on a different course. In the end, all his achievements didn't mean anything to him anymore. He admitted this, saying: "I once thought these things were valuable, but now I consider them worthless because of what Christ has done. Yes, everything else is worthless when compared with the infinite value of knowing Christ Jesus my Lord. For his sake I have discarded everything else, counting it all as garbage, so that I could gain Christ and become one with him" (Philippians 3:7–9 NLT). Paul's eyes were opened to the higher value of a relationship with Jesus Christ. He understood that apart from God, there is no true righteousness, only self-righteousness. He gained more with Christ!

Imagine how a social or business conversation would go when the only credential we talk about is being a Jesus follower. Do you think people will find us valuable or worthless? Let's try to see if we really are proud of the infinite value of knowing Jesus and becoming one with Him.

• • • • • • • • • • • • • • • • • • • •

Lord, what a blessing Paul is to us today, teaching us to understand and embrace how knowing You is what counts the most!

Secret Keeper

Wouldn't God have found this out,
since He knows the secrets of the heart?
PSALM 44:21 HCSB

The older our children get, the more secrets they have and the weightier they become. When they decide to share some of those secrets with us, it usually involves multiple assurances that we won't tell anyone. Those times with our children remind us of going the same thing as a child. Trusting someone with our biggest secrets is a huge step of faith and a sign of great friendship.

It can be hard as we get older to still have a close friend we can share anything with. Some teenage girls appear to always be scouting for information they can spread to other people or tuck away for future use. The same can also be said for many grown women.

What we learn and pass on to our children is that as much as we'd like to be their secret keeper, we're not always their best choice. We also need to realize that sometimes our children don't want to share their secrets with us or that it might be best if Mom doesn't always know every detail of their lives.

When we aren't big enough to fill that role for our children,

God is. Nothing our children can say will take God by surprise because He knows everything about every situation. They have no reason to be embarrassed or ashamed of anything they tell Him. They can talk confidently to God because nothing they say will ever go any further.

Some days we need that same assurance for ourselves, even as moms. We have feelings, dreams, or questions that we want to work through but hesitate to share for various reasons. Whatever it is, we can take it to God. He's still our number one secret keeper, just like when we were girls.

Dear God, thank You for being the secret keeper that I can talk to about anything at any time. Show me how to be just as trustworthy when my children or friends bring their secrets to me. Amen.

Aiming for Imperfection

*Not that I have already obtained this or am
already perfect, but I press on to make it my own,
because Christ Jesus has made me his own.*
PHILIPPIANS 3:12 ESV

We don't have to look very hard to see how far we are from
being an ideal woman. We slip and fumble our way through life,
with even the best days having moments we'd rather change.
Fortunately, God doesn't bless us with children and expect
us to be perfect moms. God knows we'll have days when we're
impatient or angry. We'll say things we shouldn't, forget things
we promise, and inadvertently embarrass them at times. In
other words, we approach motherhood like we did all those
years leading to that point: as perfectly imperfect.

It's time to stop getting frustrated with our shortcomings,
no matter how high society sets the bar for us as moms (or
how high we set it for ourselves). Instead, we need to celebrate our imperfections. Those hips that are wider than we'd
like bounced fussy babies countless times. Our fingernails
are ragged because we spent the afternoon planting flowers
with our children. We can barely sing the hymns on Sunday
morning because we spent Saturday night cheering at a ball

game. Those imperfections in the world's eyes add up to a perfectly good mom from God's viewpoint.

If we were picture perfect, we could fall into the trap of believing we have this mom thing figured out. We wouldn't ask for God's help or admit that we don't have all the answers. We might forget that all the aspects of motherhood are gifts from God, including the bumps along the way. And that we're only able to survive those bumps because God is leading the way.

Our perfect God trusts us, even though we are imperfect women, to take on the most important job in the world. And if God can overlook our imperfections, so should everyone else.

• •

Thank You, Lord, for trusting me
to be a mom. I'm far from perfect
and don't always do a very good job,
but I can handle anything because
You're with me. Thank You for
Your love and help. Amen.

When Opportunity Passes You By

*"There are many virtuous and capable women
in the world, but you surpass them all!"*

PROVERBS 31:29 NLT

Emily was one of three up for promotion. Because she was a mom of two young kids, with one barely a year old, her company decided to pass her up. She was told, "This job means moving to the other office, which is at least an hour's drive one way. You have two young kids and will probably have a hard time juggling work and motherhood." Emily was discouraged. After all the years of hard work, the opportunity to move up in her career was taken away from her—and all because of motherhood!

The Proverbs 31 woman is the go-to example for an ideal career mom. Her motherhood was never in the way. Here's what it says: "She finds wool and flax and busily spins it. She is like a merchant's ship, bringing her food from afar. She gets up before dawn to prepare breakfast for her household and plan the day's work for her servant girls. She goes to inspect a field and buys it; with her earnings she plants a vineyard. She

is energetic and strong, a hard worker. She makes sure her dealings are profitable; her lamp burns late into the night" (vv. 13–18 NLT).

How come the Proverbs 31 woman never struggled with wearing the two hats of motherhood and work? She didn't need to sleep in even after working late at night. Nothing seems to be too pressing in her home (she prepared breakfast and the day's schedule) or at her workplace (she went off to make purchases for her business and did her books at the end of the day). Most of us would have put off some of those things for another day, until we could get to them.

We should know that the woman's success revolved around her fear of God (v. 30). And the result of such faith? "Reward her for all she has done. Let her deeds publicly declare her praise" (v. 31 NLT). That's the abundance we see!

• •

Dear God, teach me to consider my identity in Your Son, Jesus Christ, as the best success I can have!

DAY 67

Decision Time

God uses it to prepare and equip his
people to do every good work.
2 Timothy 3:17 nlt

We begin making decisions for our children before they're born and continue for years afterward. Any subject or situation is fair game for our opinions. Our word is the final say-so more often than not. But that starts to change as our children grow older. They must learn how to process information and make decisions for themselves instead of always relying on us. We must learn how to step back, close our mouths, and only chime in when asked. This is how God intended it to be.

The Bible directs parents to "train up a child in the way he should go" (Proverbs 22:6 amp) and to "teach them diligently" (Deuteronomy 6:7 amp). We're charged with instructing our children in what they need to know to become independent, and preparing them to teach the next generation. Nothing says we should coddle our children so much they want to stay under our guidance forever.

We start with simple steps like letting our children decide which color toothbrush to bring home from the dentist. Things get more complicated as we guide them about choosing friends.

Reaching crossroads such as allowing them to switch their major halfway through college truly tests our resolve to relinquish decisions.

As difficult as those moments might be, life would be even more challenging if we didn't allow our children to take those steps. We would look back years later and realize we'd raised a mindless robot, parroting our own viewpoints. God didn't create us to never question anything or never think for ourselves. He blessed us with intelligence and insight, with bright minds made for learning. Let's have pride in our children's knowledge and pray that God will lead them to make wise decisions of their own.

• •

Dear God, it can be hard to learn how to let my children make decisions for themselves instead of always telling them what to do. Teach them to choose wisely, and teach me to give them the space to do it. Amen.

Promises, Promises

*"The promise is for you and your children and for all who
are far off—for all whom the Lord our God will call."*
ACTS 2:39 NIV

Our children use all sorts of tactics to ensure that we'll stick
to a promise, from hooking pinkie fingers to asking us to put it
in writing. We make these promises with the best intentions,
but life can set in, and circumstances can change. If we have to
break a promise, our children won't take it lightly and probably
won't forget it anytime soon. They're hurt. They're angry. We
can't blame them for reacting that way because we've been in
their position before. Whichever side of the situation we're on,
the result is the same: trust is shaken and needs to be restored.

It's nice to know that in the midst of our human failings and
shake-ups, God makes His own promises to us that will never
change and will never be broken. Let's look at a few big ones:

- God will provide everything we need (Philippians 4:19)
- God will help us get away from situations that tempt
  us too much (1 Corinthians 10:13)
- Everything in our lives works together for good when
  we love and serve God (Romans 8:28)

- God has prepared a place for us in heaven (John 14:1–3)
- God has special plans for each of us (Jeremiah 29:11)
- God will give us a type of peace that the world can't (John 14:27)
- God forgives our sins (1 John 1:9).

What a great list! As the old saying goes, we can take those promises to the bank because we know they're reliable. Anything else pales in comparison, no matter how important it might seem at the moment. Let's think about promises we've made to our children or other people lately. How can we renew our resolve to keep those promises whenever possible?

Dear God, I'm overwhelmed when I think about how many wonderful things You've promised me that reach every part of my life. Thank You for loving me enough to do that. Amen.

Lay Aside Your Burden

*"Come to me, all who labor and are heavy
laden, and I will give you rest."*
MATTHEW 11:28 ESV

"I sometimes feel burdened and lonely," a young mom said. She sees herself shouldering parenting most of the time. Even if her husband helps, she finds that most of their children's needs can be met only by her.

Let's admit that as mothers, we tend to overthink and overdo some of the parenting routines. We have our own ways of handling things when we are caring for our children. So when someone else momentarily takes over the parenting job and the performance does not meet our standards, we step in and claim the job back. No wonder we are burdened and feel lonely in our parenting journey!

Jesus calls us with these words: "Come to me, all who labor and are heavy laden, and I will give you rest. Take my yoke upon you, and learn from me, for I am gentle and lowly in heart, and you will find rest for your souls. For my yoke is easy, and my burden is light" (Matthew 11:28–30 ESV).

Here's a picture to illustrate the passage for us. Jesus says, "I want to give you a ride so you don't have to walk, especially

with that heavy purse." You get in the car with Him, and you fasten your seat belt, but your purse is still hanging on your shoulder. Then Jesus reminds you, "You will be more comfortable during the ride if you lay your purse aside." But you don't want to, so you shrug your shoulders and insist that you are comfortable. Are you really? It would be a more pleasant ride if you were free from the hanging purse!

Moms, a beautiful invitation from Jesus has been extended to us! Today we are being asked to lay aside our burdens, how we manage ourselves, and our parenting expectations. And if someone offers you a self-care day, take it. It's okay to have help, even to ask for it. A well-deserved rest will help you recharge and refocus!

• •

Lord, let me not be too preoccupied
with my expectations that I am
burdened with parenting.

145

Butterfly Basking

Seek the LORD and his strength;
seek his presence continually!
1 CHRONICLES 16:11 ESV

The butterfly perched near the playground slide, not seeming to be bothered much by Sarah's daughter as she ran and jumped. It flitted back and forth to other places a few times when Emma got too close, but it always returned to the spot by the slide, regally opening and closing its wings in a steady rhythm.

Emma was thrilled by the glimpses of orange, blue, and yellow on the butterfly's dusky black wings. She was even more fascinated when her mom explained the purpose of its exercise: to absorb enough of the sun's heat to continue flying later.

As Sarah watched Emma play, she also kept a check on the butterfly. She thought of how its attention to and appreciation of the sun was remarkable considering the nearby activity and noise. She admired its tenacity for repeatedly circling back to its favored spot.

We need to be like the butterfly, though the Son we need to pay attention to and worship—Jesus—is much more than the sun the butterfly sought. Jesus was there when God put the sun, moon, and stars in place. He was there when every

butterfly was created and painted with God's hand.

The butterfly is naturally drawn to the sun, returning repeatedly and depending on it for survival. We should also be drawn to God and return to Him when life knocks us off our path. Some days it's easy to say we automatically turn to God. Other days we can't say that, when so many other things seem to take over the day before it even starts. God knows this about us, and fortunately understands. He's always waiting whenever we turn our faces back to Him to bask in His glory and love. . .just like a butterfly.

• •

Lord God, there's so much I can learn
about You through the things I see
in nature. Give me the desire to focus
on You every day, just like a butterfly
seeks out the sun. Amen.

The Best Job

Whatever your hands find to do,
do with all your strength.
ECCLESIASTES 9:10 HCSB

A debate surrounds every mom at one time or another, even if we'd like to steer clear: is it better for our children if we choose to stay at home with them or if we work outside the home? Whichever position we're in, we can be torn between the possibilities. Moms who stay home spend more day-to-day face time with their children. Moms who work outside the home have less time with their children each day, but it might be higher quality because they want to make every minute count. Both options have pros and cons. Both can work well for a family. Neither makes us a better or worse mom, no matter what supporters of one option versus the other might say.

God wants us to help care for our families in the best way possible, whichever position we're in. The Bible tells of women who apparently stayed at home with their families (like Jesus' mother, Mary), women who had businesses of their own (such as Lydia in Acts 16:11–15), and women who worked inside the home but also helped provide the family's income (see Proverbs 31).

Having so many examples to learn from shows us that any

combination of motherhood and work can be a blessing to us and our families. As long as we pray about the decision and ask God to help us keep things in balance, God will honor that desire and show us what to do. That doesn't always mean we'll follow one path forever. God might have different plans for us in a few years. Let's commit to doing our best job as a mom wherever we are and supporting all the mothers we know, whatever their jobs might be. We might just find ourselves switching places someday.

• •

Dear Lord, whether You want me to stay at home or work somewhere else, the most important job You gave me is as a mom. Help me to focus on that so that I can give my best to my family, wherever I am. Thank You. Amen.

Limited Edition

"I have loved you with an everlasting love;
therefore I have continued my faithfulness to you."
JEREMIAH 31:3 ESV

She was finally going to experience being a mom to a daughter. . .and she was excited! Although they were bringing her stepdaughter home because of health issues, she was also looking forward to being a confidant and an advocate. But the diagnosis for the young woman's medical condition was permanent, affecting her ability to get a job. It started to put a strain on her marriage. So the best thing to do was to purchase an airline ticket to ship her stepdaughter off to a friend and give her money for the next couple of months.

How interesting to note that excitement can turn into a nightmare for us moms (and stepmoms) when the going gets tough! Is it for show that we take on responsibility but decide to quit when we can no longer handle the heat? When conversations start sounding like a broken record, we realize that our counsel falls on deaf ears and we're back to square one. We're fed up! What happened to loving without limits?

The Bible always talks about God's unconditional love. We seem to understand the concept very well when it's directed

at us. We relish the idea of the God of second chances, because it provides us the opportunity to start all over again when we make a mistake. . .when we sin. But the instruction to love the same way God loves us? We are all words without action!

"I have loved you with an everlasting love; therefore I have continued my faithfulness to you," God said to Israel. The verse didn't say God loved Israel yesterday. It said "everlasting"—always.

And because His love is everlasting, He also promised Israel, "Again I will build you, and you shall be built" (Jeremiah 31:4 ESV). God did not say, "Here's an airline ticket and some money. Go and start your own life!" God Himself is the one doing the building, not from a distance, but right where we are. And He makes sure that we get to a better place.

• •

Thank You, Father, for Your everlasting love and for not quitting on us!

151

Fresh Starts

Be kind to each other, tenderhearted, forgiving one another, just as God through Christ has forgiven you.
EPHESIANS 4:32 NLT

"I'm sorry" can be one of the most difficult phrases for our children to learn to say—or for us to say ourselves. Equally difficult can be the companion response "It's okay. I forgive you." The words are simple but carry tremendous weight. They're the first small steps toward repairing a damaged ego or smoothing away anger. They're what we need to say and hear before we can regroup and start fresh.

Forgiveness is a two-way prospect. Some days we need to recognize our fault and humble ourselves to ask for forgiveness, even of our children. Other days we need to show mercy and forgive them when they ask for it. Jesus taught that the best place to start forgiving someone is by realizing how much forgiveness we need ourselves. It's not hard to do. When we stop to think about how many times we do or say things we shouldn't, the list of what we need forgiveness for quickly grows.

Here's the other part of the equation that's equally important. Before we ask God to forgive us for things, Jesus taught that we need to be sure we aren't withholding forgiveness

from someone else. We start the process of being forgiven by showing mercy and love to the people around us. Then, once those personal situations are resolved, we can boldly ask for God's forgiveness ourselves.

Since we moms are far from perfect, on most days we'll have plenty of opportunities to request forgiveness. We'll also get lots of practice sharing forgiveness since our children aren't exactly perfect either. Through both sides of the experience, we see how God draws us closer to Him and to our children. Let's be sure to thank God for that today.

• •

Lord, You would think I'd be better at asking for forgiveness by now as much as I need it. Thank You for always forgiving me. Help me to use it as a reminder for how I need to always forgive others. Amen.

DAY 74

Keeping in Touch

The eyes of the LORD are on the righteous,
and His ears are open to their cry for help.
PSALM 34:15 HCSB

No matter how old our children get or how independent we encourage them to be, we're leery of completely cutting the infamous apron strings. We want them to keep in touch with us, even if it's only a quick text or email to let us know they're okay and that they're thinking of us. It's easy to see that need from our mom perspective and to feel justified in getting frustrated or having our feelings hurt when our children don't communicate as often as we'd like.

Let's flip the roles and look at it as if we're the child reaching out to the parent instead of being the parent waiting on the child. Whether our earthly parents are still here for us to talk to or not, we have a heavenly Father who's always available.

We know how much we love our own children and that God loves us infinitely more. As much as we long to hear from our children and find joy in the smallest connection, God also longs to hear from us and finds pleasure in whatever we bring to Him. Numerous verses in the Bible tell of how God listens to our cries, hears our prayers, and wants us to come to Him.

God wouldn't teach that He's always listening if He weren't ready for us to talk!

Everything we think or feel is valid conversation with God. Little things, like "Good morning." Big things, like "Show me which decision is right." In-between things, like "Help my children have a good day." If that sounds like the kinds of conversations we like to have with our children, it should. Let's always talk with our children but not forget to talk with God. Anything at anytime—that's when God invites us to share with Him.

• •

Lord, thank You for always being ready to listen to me. Forgive me for the times when I don't talk to You as often, and help me to back on track. Show me if there are ways I can communicate better with my children too. Amen.

You Have Your Own Special Place

Having gifts that differ according to the
grace given to us, let us use them.
ROMANS 12:6 ESV

A working mom wanted to volunteer for the booster clubs of her daughters but was hesitant to sign up for the jobs available. She felt she wouldn't be able to do anything until she creatively thought of ways to help. Reluctantly she offered, "I can buy the stamps, stick them on the envelopes, and mail them." It took the stress off another mom doing multiple things. And then, "I can man the snack table at 6:00 p.m. every other Wednesday." The booster now had a permanent mom for one shift. She *was* able to participate!

We sometimes exclude ourselves from being part of something because we compare ourselves to others. We think we lack time and abilities to contribute as we watch other moms happily shuttling their kids to every game and activity. They always have team spirit to cheer on their teams. And whatever coaches need, they're on it!

At home, we talk about family teamwork and ask every

member to discover how to help one another and work as a unit. We sign up our kids for sports, where they learn more about teamwork. The coach assigns individual positions but encourages them to communicate and to work cohesively. The workforce considers the strengths of team members, aligns them accordingly with responsibilities, and tells them to collaborate.

The Bible also stresses the importance of working together. The body of Christ is made up of individuals with different characteristics and various gifts. In the book of Romans, we read, "Having gifts that differ according to the grace given to us, let us use them: if prophecy, in proportion to our faith; if service, in our serving; the one who teaches, in his teaching; the one who exhorts, in his exhortation; the one who contributes, in generosity; the one who leads, with zeal; the one who does acts of mercy, with cheerfulness" (12:6–8 ESV).

Rejoice, for there is a special place reserved for each one of us! There is a role that we can play, that is just as important for collective success. We are better when united!

• •

What a blessing, Lord, to know that You have equipped me so that I can work with others!

Every Child Should Belong

*"Should we accept only good things from the
hand of God and never anything bad?"*
JOB 2:10 NLT

Her daughter was born with Down syndrome. On top of her difficulty accepting her daughter's condition, she suffered from an undiagnosed and untreated postpartum depression, which was dismissed as a phase all moms go through after childbirth. It was all too much, and she had a nervous breakdown. She was never able to care for her daughter.

Part of the Serenity Prayer says, "to accept the things I cannot change." It's a known fact that we are very good at attempting to change everything except our own selves. But what do we do when our child is diagnosed with a disability and there is nothing that can reverse it? How easy is it to accept that our child will be different from others? It is hard to see our visions of our child's future just taken away. Hard as it may be, every child—including one with a disability—should belong.

From a spiritual standpoint, we cannot think of a disability as a punishment from God. We also shouldn't curse God because of it. We need to re-examine our beliefs, not just individually but as a family. As Job aptly asked, "Should we accept only

good things from the hand of God and never anything bad?" No! The best thing we can do is to remember that "God is our refuge and strength" (Psalm 46:1 NLT).

From a practical perspective, the most effective support system for our children, with or without disability, begins with us moms. We should be the best educators and advocates for them. The sooner we learn what appropriate programs are available and how best we can be part of the developmental training, the more benefits we can reap for them and the rest of our family.

It is also good to find our own support group. Reaching out to other moms to share our journeys will encourage us. And if we need professional counsel, let's find someone who can help break things down. The bottom line is to accept the beauty of caring for our special child and to believe that every child belongs!

● ●

You have given me a special child to love and nurture. Help me to know what I need to do.

Green-Eyed Monsters

Do not worship any other god, for the LORD,
whose name is Jealous, is a jealous God.
EXODUS 34:14 NIV

As exhausting as the early months of motherhood might be, they bring a sweet reward: our babies see us as the center of their worlds, the person they depend on most for whatever they need. Things change, though, as our children get older and trust more people.

We can experience a rude awakening when we realize we're no longer the automatic center of our child's world. Another shock runs through us when our children reach the age of consciously choosing their friends over us. The green-eyed monster we might not have seen lately rears its head and mocks us. We're jealous that we're no longer first in our children's hearts.

Earthly jealousy—wanting something we can't have—isn't a good thing. Holy jealousy, however, can be a different matter. Holy jealousy stems from being possessive of something that's rightfully ours. We might not stop to think about it very often, but God experiences holy jealousy toward us. God created us that so we could have an intimate relationship with Him. We

belong to God, which means He is the only rightful recipient of our love. When we turn away from God or put other things ahead of Him, God is jealous. The jealousy isn't because God is insecure in any way. It's proof of His love for us.

Think about it. We don't get jealous about things we don't care about. God loves us deeply and wants us to love Him. He takes His love seriously and expects us to do the same. Jealousy and love are intertwined, whether we're pondering our relationship with our children or with God. It's wise to get rid of any human jealousy lurking in our hearts so that we can turn our children completely over to God in order to focus more fully on Him.

• •

Lord, it's strange to think that You could love me enough to be jealous for me, but I'm glad that You do. Bring me closer to You so that You don't have a reason to miss my love and be jealous. Amen.

No More Excuses

But Moses said, "Pardon your servant,
Lord. Please send someone else."
EXODUS 4:13 NIV

"I'm too tall." "I'm too short." "I'm not smart enough." "I don't know how." "I forgot." Such are the litany of excuses we hear from our children when they fall short of the mark. Sometimes they accept responsibility themselves, but the blame often shifts to someone else's shoulders. We can tire of the excuses, especially when we're pinpointed as the bad guy in a situation that was out of our control.

Though no situation is ever out of His control, God may also get tired of hearing excuses, such as "I don't know enough about the Bible to teach anyone," or "Approaching that homeless person would make me feel uncomfortable," or "No one would want me to fix them dinner because I'm not a very good cook." If we stop between excuses long enough to wait for God's response, we might hear something along the lines of *"Who cares? Give it a try, and trust Me to make it happen."*

The Bible relates many situations where God instructed people to do things they weren't used to doing and weren't necessarily qualified for. Things such as moving to hostile

countries, approaching kings with drastic demands, and fighting armies of countless soldiers. Some people tried to make excuses and escape those assignments, but God countered the objections and showed them how they could be accomplished with His help.

God does the same for us. If we believe God wants us to try something different, then we need to trust that He'll help us do it. Asking questions is fine, but giving countless excuses is not. We just need to tell God "yes" and take the first step. He will handle the rest.

● ●

Thank You, God, for asking me to do things for You. Stop me from focusing on my own limitations when I'm afraid to try. Teach me to trust You to get the job done once I take the first step. Amen.

Tantrum Time

*Oh, that I had one to hear me! (Here is my
signature! Let the Almighty answer me!)*
JOB 31:35 ESV

One moment ranks high on every mom's list of least favorite memories: the first time one of our children had a temper tantrum in public. We teach our children to be on their best behavior at school, in church, and any other time they're away from home. But none of us can be depended on to follow all the rules, especially young children.

Everyone needs an escape, a safe place to go when they feel like throwing a tantrum—a place where we know we are unconditionally loved. That safe place for many of us is home. As painful as the fights can be, we moms want our children to feel that way, to know that they can unpack their feelings around us and everything will be okay.

We need to do the same thing ourselves, though as parents we don't always want our children to know the things on our minds or the issues we're tackling. That's when we turn to God as our safe place, our no-holds-barred zone where we can even dare to throw our own tantrum on occasion. Stories throughout the Bible tell us about people who shared their negative feelings

164

with God, particularly in the Psalms. Anger, frustration, fear, disbelief, abandonment, jealousy, hatred—they're all right there for us to read and relate to.

The beauty from our perspective is that God actually invites us to bring these things to Him. Nothing we say, no accusations we make, will reduce God to being less than all powerful. Nothing will make God turn away or cover His ears and refuse to listen. We all have times when frustrations build up inside us, just waiting for escape. Isn't it nice to know we can tell them to God, no matter how they might sound? He's big enough to handle it.

• •

Dear God, as much as I try to teach my children not to lose control of their anger, sometimes I need the release myself. Thank You for letting me know I can free myself by dumping it all on You. Amen.

165

Falling Fruit

*"I am the vine; you are the branches. If you
remain in me and I in you, you will bear much
fruit; apart from me you can do nothing."*
JOHN 15:5 NIV

"The apple doesn't fall far from the tree," the old saying goes, reminding us that our families and environment help shape who we are. As our children grow, we can see how closely they resemble us, from physical appearance and mannerisms to attitudes and beliefs. Our hope is that they reflect the more positive aspects of our lives instead of the negative.

Jesus is the perfect "tree" for us to come from and remain close to. He compared Himself to a vine, with the people who loved and believed in Him as the branches (see John 15:5). Each branch has the freedom to grow and produce fruit but will only live if it stays attached to the vine. We are the branches on God's vine. When we trust God and keep our relationship with Him going, we'll learn and grow strong. We'll bear fruit by doing the things God wants us to do.

If we slip away from God and try to get through life on our own, it will be as if someone has cut us from the vine. We'll wither spiritually and emotionally, dry up, and die. Fortunately,

we have an advantage over actual vines and branches. Cutting ourselves off from God doesn't mean we're permanently abandoned with no future hope. We can return to God and reestablish our connection. He's always willing to graft us back to the vine.

We also can bear fruit for God again. This fruit often will be more valuable than our earlier offerings because we have a better understanding of how important our relationship with God is. We serve others more willingly and look for more opportunities to use the talents God has given us. Here's to a fresh harvest that falls close to the tree.

• •

Dear God, I want to stay connected to You and get my life from You just like a branch does from the tree. Help me to produce abundant fruit that falls so close to You that there's no doubt who I'm serving. Amen.

Gossip Girls

*Do not let any unwholesome talk come out of your mouths,
but only what is helpful for building others up according
to their needs, that it may benefit those who listen.*
EPHESIANS 4:29 NIV

One of the many things that sets us women apart from men
is our desire for details. We want to know who's doing what,
where, and why. Seeing two friends whispering sends our
minds in dozens of directions as we try to guess what they're
discussing. Some days we're the ones whispering and spreading
information. It's a situation we can find ourselves in repeatedly,
even though we know being the news-sharer might come back
to haunt us.

How do we get a grip on the gossip? More importantly,
how do we teach our children to? It's human nature to want
acceptance. Seeing ourselves as the person others consider to
be "in the know" can make us feel accepted, no matter our age.
Those are important things to acknowledge to ourselves and
with our children. But God doesn't love or accept people who
know the latest news any more than anyone else.

God teaches us specific things about gossip, and they're not
very good. The Bible says that people who gossip separate close

friends (see Proverbs 16:28), are fools (see Proverbs 10:18), and have religion that means nothing (see James 1:26). Ouch! That's not the group we want to be part of, and we don't want our children there either. Instead, we want to be the people who encourage others with our words and say the kinds of things we hope people would say about us.

Let's make a deal with our children for the days when it seems like we'll explode if we keep our mouths shut: tell it to God. The words won't hurt anyone, won't travel any further, and won't be something we could regret later. Plus, because God already knows the situation, He won't even be shocked. He's the best "gossip partner" around.

Lord, You know how hard it can be for me to keep things to myself. Show me when I'm crossing the line from regular conversation to gossip. Help me to honor people with my words, not spread rumors or tear people down. Thank You. Amen.

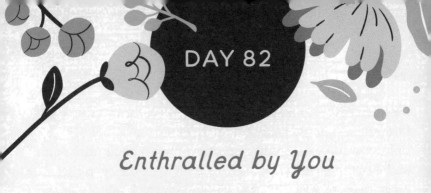

Enthralled by You

Let the king be enthralled by your beauty;
honor him, for he is your lord.
Psalm 45:11 niv

When our babies are born, we can't get enough of them. Their tiny presence holds sway over us, and we'll do anything for them. We spend hours gazing at them, marveling at how amazing and perfect they are. Just thinking about them makes our hearts swell and brings a smile. We're absolutely enthralled. How often do we remind ourselves that God feels the same way about us?

Psalm 45 tells of a king's wedding as an illustration of our relationship with God. It's a wonderful celebration with both the bride and groom excited about the day. And the king isn't just in love with his bride-to-be. He's enthralled by her. Definitions for the word *enthralled* include phrases such as "to fascinate," "to capture," "charmed," and "to hold as if in a spell." When the verse says that the king is enthralled by the bride's beauty, it's telling how God feels about us.

God doesn't just like us; He's enchanted by us. God doesn't just have a passing interest in our lives; He's spellbound by everything we do. And God doesn't just half listen to our prayers

while He handles other business; God is fascinated by every word we say.

It can be hard for us to believe that anyone—and especially God—could ever be enthralled with us once we moved past our own baby stage. But it's true. The God of the universe, the God who put the planets in motion, the God who created everything in and under heaven, the God who knows every person by name and counts the number of hairs on our heads—that same God is fascinated by us. Captivated. Enthralled by our beauty. How amazing is that?

• •

Lord, I don't know why You're fascinated
with me, but I'm glad You are. Thank You
for loving me and for being my King.
Teach me to honor You in everything I do. Amen.

Childlike Trust

Truly I say to you, unless you repent (change, turn about)
and become like little children [trusting, lowly, loving,
forgiving], you can never enter the kingdom of heaven [at all].
MATTHEW 18:3 AMPC

Life is so simple for our babies. We fix their food, rock them
to sleep, and take them where they need to be. Yes, as they get
older they fight over toys and don't always want to do what we
say, but overall life with little ones is good. We could learn a
lot from our children at that stage, when they're still innocent
and trusting instead of worldly and harried.

Jesus spent time with children and invited them to come
closer instead of hanging on the fringes of the crowd like
they'd been taught to do. Then Jesus surprised the adults even
more by using the children as an example. Jesus taught that
if we want to live with Him in heaven someday, we need to
be like children again. Being responsible adults is important
and has its place in this world, but it is not the only thing
that matters.

Children are special because of their innocence, absolute
trust, and uncomplicated love for other people. They believe
the adult who promises to take care of them, and they don't

worry about things once that adult is in control. That's how God wants us to be with Him. God wants us to love Him with certainty and without any strings attached. To believe Him when He promises to take care of us. To give Him all our problems and questions and ask Him to take care of things.

Rediscovering how to approach life with childlike trust and love sounds crazy on the surface but is the most rewarding thing we'll ever do when we put our trust in God. We spend years teaching our children how to love, and God does the same for us. We can trust Him with everything for a lifetime.

• •

Dear Lord, thank You for inviting me to come near, just like Jesus did with the children in the crowd. Show me how to love and trust You like an innocent child who knows You're in control. Amen.

Forever Mom

> *"I am the Alpha and the Omega," says the Lord God,*
> *"who is, and who was, and who is to come, the Almighty."*
> REVELATION 1:8 NIV

No matter how old our children get or how grown up they might be in the world's eyes, two things never change: we'll always be Mom, and they'll always be our babies. That's because the cartoon that sometimes circulates around Mother's Day is true. When we take on the job of motherhood, we go into it knowing there will never be any official holidays or vacations for longer than a few days. We also know that being Mom is a lifetime position, not something we'll retire from in fifteen or twenty years.

Our "forever Mom" status is a reflection of God's presence and power. We're Mom from the day we have a positive pregnancy test until we take our last breath. God is always God, in every situation, through all time. Nothing we can do or say will change who God is. He is all powerful and all knowing. Turning away and ignoring God might mean we don't see Him very clearly, but it doesn't change the fact that He's still there.

God calls Himself the Alpha and the Omega (see Revelation 1:8), which are the first and last letters of the Greek alphabet.

They mean "beginning" and "end." The title applies because God was here in the beginning when He formed everything and will be here at the end when everything is finished. God is here for every minute in between, however many years that will be.

On those days when it seems like being a forever mom is too much to handle, remember God is with us every step of the way—through eternity, as a matter of fact. When we close our eyes and turn to Him, our forever God will encourage and support us as only He can.

• •

Dear God, it's hard to wrap my mind around the concept that You're truly the Alpha and Omega, the beginning and end. But whether I understand it or not, I'm glad it's true. Thank You for being here and for helping me be the best forever mom I can. Amen.

New Perspectives

*If anyone is in Christ, he is a new creation; old things
have passed away, and look, new things have come.*
2 Corinthians 5:17 HCSB

We see things differently as we age or as we gain wisdom
through new experiences. For many women, few things change
our perspective on life as much (or as quickly) as motherhood.
The music or movies we've enjoyed for years suddenly seem
more "in your face" than we'd realized before our toddler's ears
were tuned in. Shopping after work is less appealing because
we want our children to be at home and safe instead of out and
about after dark.

Our perspectives also change because of our relationships with God. The closer we become to God, the more He
changes our thoughts, feelings, and attitudes to reflect His.
The changes start on the inside and work their way out, until
the people around us notice the difference.

The things we used to focus on might not seem very important anymore (much like when we become moms). Things that
the world expects or accepts without question seem off-kilter
when we look at them through God's eyes. Realizing that we're
changing can be a shock, but it's okay. Seeing things from God's

perspective and reacting the way He wants us to is how we know we're becoming a new person.

New perspectives are crisp, clean, and perfect. They're ready to be used for whatever purpose they were created and enjoyed by the people who use them. That's exactly how we are when God takes away our old self (including our perspective on things) and replaces it with the new. We're clean and perfect, ready for a fresh start that follows God's plan. God created us for a purpose and is molding us to be the perfect woman for the job. Whatever that purpose might be, let's thank God today for the new women He's creating in us.

• •

Thank You, Lord, for making me into the person You want me to be. Give me patience as You change me from the inside out, because I know it won't happen overnight. I want to be used for You. Amen.

DAY 86

Everyday Thanks

*At all times and for everything giving thanks in the
name of our Lord Jesus Christ to God the Father.*
EPHESIANS 5:20 AMPC

It can be easy to garner thanks when we do something big for our children, like pick them up when they have car trouble or surprise them with extra spending money. Those thank-yous warm us inside, but the best ones are for the routine jobs or the small things we happen to think about and do because we're Mom. When our children thank us for those things, it shows that they noticed we went out of our way to do something extra. God just might feel the same way about our thanks to Him.

We remember to thank God for big things He's done or for prayers we know He's answered: safety when our children travel during a storm, the healing of a friend or family member, a job situation that works out in our favor. We also might have a litany of items we thank God for every day: our family, a job that helps pay the bills, food, and clothing. But how often do our thanks bubble to the surface for the small things, the things that are easily unnoticed?

Everything we have is a gift from God. The air we breathe, the physical strength to get out of bed and go through our

day, the patterns of sunshine filtering through trees along the road. It's right to give God thanks for all these things, but let's challenge ourselves to pay special attention to the small ones. A simple way to make that happen is to start writing down the small things we want to thank God for in a day or a week. When we start to look, God might surprise us with how quickly our list grows.

• •

Thank You, Lord, for all the things You give me and all the things You do for me. There's no way I could ever list them all, but please make me more aware so that I can at least be more grateful. Amen.

179

Sharing Spotlights

Humble yourselves, therefore, under the mighty hand
of God so that at the proper time he may exalt you.
1 PETER 5:6 ESV

Sharing the spotlight can come naturally for some of us (and our children) who prefer to stay in the background without drawing too much attention to ourselves. For spotlight seekers, however, learning to let others "have their moment" can be a hard step to take.

Life is full of situations that help us teach our children this lesson. A new student ends our child's three-year reign as spelling bee champ. Another kid lands the lead role our teenager hoped for in the community theater's production. A coworker takes credit for work on a special project. We have to learn to step aside gracefully, which only comes with practice. And as important as that lesson might be, there's a bigger issue at stake for us and our children.

How willingly do we share the stage of our life with God? Are we okay with the idea of God "stealing our thunder" and being in control? Here's the truth that sometimes gets buried beneath the busyness of life: God is in control, regardless of whether we like to admit it. God always has the spotlight and

controls where it shines, even if it momentarily shines on us.

We might be listed as the conference planner, but God gave us the organizational and administrative skills for the job. Our cakes might be the top draw at the annual bake sale, but our love for cooking and our decorating skills came from God. No matter what our initial response to being in the spotlight might be, God can help us keep it in perspective. Everything we're able to do and every bit of praise we get for it is because of God. Next time, let's officially invite Him to join us in the spotlight and see how much more we enjoy it.

• • • • • • • • • • • • • • • • • • • •

Dear God, I know that anytime I'm in the spotlight, it's really because of You. I can only do things worth getting attention because You help me to do them. Teach me to keep it in perspective and use those times as a chance to praise You. Amen.

181

Adopted through Love

God decided in advance to adopt us into his own family by bringing us to himself through Jesus Christ. This is what he wanted to do, and it gave him great pleasure.
EPHESIANS 1:5 NLT

Every child is special and hopefully is loved and treasured by family and friends. But people sometimes think the relationship between a parent and child is even more special when that child is adopted.

If we're Mom to our own biological children, our pregnancy might have been well planned, or it might have been a surprise. Moms of adopted children step into the world of motherhood with full knowledge of where they're going. Adoptions aren't accidental. The parents want a child and go through the adoption process to make it happen. Enduring months—or even years—of making decisions, meeting with people, filling out papers, and waiting for answers isn't an easy task. The parents do it because they want to. They want a child to call their own and take intentional steps to get there.

God looks at us the same way. Children don't force parents to adopt them, and we don't have to force ourselves on God. He knows us before we're born and chooses to love and accept

us just as we are. He's already waiting for us with open arms, waiting to call us "daughter." When we decide to love and follow Jesus, God adopts us into a special family. We join a group of believers who are flawed and imperfect but try to do what God wants and to show that love to others. Believers who know God and accept His love for them.

No matter how wonderful our real-life family on earth might be, our adoptive one through Jesus is infinitely better. Why? Because it's the hallmark of acceptance by God, just because of who we are and thanks to who He is. What a gift it is to be adopted!

• • • • • • • • • • • • • • • • • • •

Dear God, thank You so much for loving and adopting me into Your family. Show me how to be a valuable member of that family by helping others and teaching them about You. Amen.

Desiring God's Things

Delight yourself in the Lord, and he will
give you the desires of your heart.
PSALM 37:4 ESV

We want the best things possible for our children, from before they're born on through adulthood. We do what we can to steer them toward reliable friends, a well-rounded education, steady employment, and a loving spouse because we see those things as important. Ideally, our children share our viewpoint and want things that could help them later in life. As we teach them about goal setting and striving for great things, let's also teach them about aligning their goals with God's.

We know from verses throughout the Bible that God desires to give us those things we desire. That prospect can be very appealing. But the lesson we need to teach our children—and learn ourselves—is that having our desires fulfilled isn't as simple as telling God what we want and getting an automatic "yes." The Bible tells us that we are first to delight ourselves in the Lord.

When we delight ourselves in the Lord, we find our happiness in Him. We love, trust, and want to follow God. We realize how important prayer and Bible study are and begin to crave

time for both. We find that God can help us deal with situations much better than we might have done on our own. As we make these changes in our lives, God is pleased and wants to give us more good things in return. The interesting thing is that as we learn to delight ourselves in God, some of the things we want for ourselves—or our children—can change.

Walking with God means that our desires begin to line up with God's. That makes it easy for God to give things back to us, because we want the same things He wants for us. It's a definite win-win!

• •

Lord, I want to find my delight in You and to be satisfied with You more than anything else. Thank You for all the good things You have in store for me when I follow the path You have in mind. Amen.

185

Pretty Pictures

The whole earth is filled with awe at your
wonders; where morning dawns, where
evening fades, you call forth songs of joy.
PSALM 65:8 NIV

Our children bring home so many paintings, pictures, and craft projects over the years that we could never keep them all. We hold on for a while but eventually reach the point of going through and culling out our favorite pieces. Something about each of the "keepers" makes it special to us. Maybe we love the colors or the artistry or the associated memories. Just looking at it can warm our hearts and bring a smile to our faces, even years later.

God also paints pictures for us, and they're the best kind of all: Ones that will always be with us and make us smile when we take the time to notice. Ones that won't fade away or need to be trashed because we've surpassed our storage limit. God paints a sunrise to begin each of our days, spilling color and light across our paths. He creates patterns of leaves, twigs, and grass at our feet. Wildflowers, birds, and butterflies explode in every color of the spectrum. A television documentary reminds us of the strength and majesty

in God's creatures. The roll and roar of ocean waves draw us near and tickle our toes with foam. Mountains and cliffs stand impenetrable, stretching to meet wispy clouds and sky.

We try to capture the beauty with cameras, paints, and computer technology. The final product might earn a place on our wall or refrigerator, just as our children's artwork does. But no matter how attractive our renditions might be, nothing we make can compare with God's nature. Our versions are still only shadows of the originals. Just as our children's "keepers" remind us of their innocence and beauty, God's masterpieces remind us that He is the Great Creator of all things.

• •

Lord, You are the most amazing artist of all. Thank You for surrounding me every day with the beauty of creation. Help me to never grow tired of enjoying Your pictures. Amen.

Sweet-Smelling Prayers

Accept my prayer as incense offered to you,
and my upraised hands as an evening offering.
PSALM 141:2 NLT

Nothing else in this world smells like a baby with its combination of powders, lotions, and fabric softener layering over the scents of everyday life. The smell of our children is one of the sweetest we'll ever know, once we become a mom.

Scents are important to God too according to the Bible. When God directed His people, the Israelites, to build their first place of worship, it was a tentlike structure that could be packed up and easily moved while they traveled through the desert. Every detail of this tabernacle (and later, the temple) was important, from the colors and materials used to the ceremonies carried out by the priests to the rich scents coming from the altar of incense.

Twice each day, a priest took some coals from the altar of sacrifice to the altar of incense. A special type of incense used only in the tabernacle was placed on the coals and burned. God told the people that the incense fumes represented their prayers to Him. God was pleased with the fragrant offering

and accepted their prayers because the people were following His will.

The earthly tabernacle no longer exists. Instead, God says that we are the temple of the Holy Spirit who dwells within us. Our prayers are the sweet smell of His children coming before Him, and they please Him when our hearts are in the right place. God soaks up the offering and will never forget any prayer we bring to Him, just as we never forget breathing in the special scent of our children.

Snuggling with babies and breathing in that one-of-a-kind scent is a sweet chance to remember our own children at that age. Hopefully, it will also remind us how God is waiting to enjoy and accept our one-of-a-kind prayers.

• •

Thank You, Lord, for always being
ready to hear and accept my prayers.
May they be a sweet offering to You
just like the special incense You taught
the Israelites to make. Amen.

All Mine

*The earth is the Lord's, and everything
in it, the world, and all who live in it.*
PSALM 24:1 NIV

If we had a nickel for every time we heard one of our children claim, "Mine!" we might have quite a start on their college funds by the time they finish elementary school. No one thinks much of their behavior since it's normal for children to be over-possessive of certain things. They hopefully move through that phase without too many problems and learn that they can't claim every attractive object as their own.

Some things, however, do belong to us—but in another sense they don't. We have jobs and earn paychecks, so we are able to buy things for ourselves and our families. The house is ours because we signed a mortgage and pay the note each month. The clothes, sports equipment, and other things we use belong to us because we bought them or received them as gifts. But let's think about that for a moment.

King David wrote in Psalms that the earth and everything in it belongs to God. We understand that wild animals, oceans, and other parts of nature are God's. But sometimes we can forget that "everything" also means our everyday possessions. The material things that make up our modern society all come from resources God provided. Realizing this puts a new perspective on the "all mine" syndrome.

Everything we have is a gift from God because God created it. He gives the gifts to us freely and wants us to enjoy them, but He also wants us to remember how we got them. As we teach our children about ownership and possessions, let's not forget the most important owner of all. And when we remember, let's take it as a chance to thank God anew for the many ways He blesses us.

• •

Thank You, Lord, for all the things
You give me, especially the things
You allow me to temporarily own.
Help me to remember that everything
really belongs to You and that I
need to thank You for those
things every day. Amen.

Shifting Responsibilities

*"Arise, for it is your task, and we
are with you; be strong and do it."*
EZRA 10:4 ESV

"Mom, I've got this." "Don't worry about it." How many times have we heard these words of assurance from our children? The older they get and the more confident they become in their own abilities, the more certain they are that they can handle things alone.

That confidence might make us cringe because we can anticipate their probable mistakes and don't want to see them get hurt. We'd rather put our hand on their shoulders and keep pointing them on the paths we think are best. We certainly don't want them repeating some of our own mistakes. The reality, however, is that we can't always be with our children or give them advice. They have to learn to make decisions and be responsible for themselves. From our parenting viewpoint, we have to learn to see them as maturing adults who are capable of making their own decisions, just as God allows us to do.

God knows everything about us and our world because He created and loves us. It would be simple for God to decide

what He wants us to do and not give us any other options so that we'd be forced to go in that direction. It doesn't work that way though. God gives us minds to use and the ability to gain knowledge so that we can make wise decisions. As we grow in years and hopefully grow closer to God, we learn to ask for His guidance, whether we're stuck between two choices or taking on new responsibilities. We're advised to do exactly that, actually (see James 1:5).

Just as God allows us to learn from our mistakes and become more mature, we need to give our children those same opportunities. What's one way we can help our children grow in responsibility?

• •

Lord, it can be so hard to step back and let my children make their own decisions or try to prove they can handle more responsibilities. Show me how to support them, and remind me that You're supporting us all. Amen.

A Mother's Love

"As a mother comforts her child, so will I comfort
you; and you will be comforted over Jerusalem."
ISAIAH 66:13 NIV

The word *love* is used in so many situations most days that it can be heard in reference to anything from shoes or food to the weather, people, or God. One connotation that remains universal, however, is when we think of a mother's love for her children.

Nothing else is like the love between a mother and her children. It grows during our pregnancy and bursts into bloom for all the world to see the moment our children are born. They capture our hearts and steal them forever. Love for our children guides many of our decisions and actions for years to come.

Most Bible verses that reference God's love refer to Him as our Father. But a few compare God's love to that of a mother, illustrating in a different way just how deep and caring God's feelings for us are. These verses promise that God will always show compassion toward us and will never forget us, just as a mother cannot forget her nursing child (see Isaiah 49:15); God will comfort us as a mother does her child (see Isaiah 66:13); God will protect us as a mother eagle or

194

mother bear protects her young (see Deuteronomy 32:11–12 and Hosea 13:8).

Jesus compared Himself to a mother hen when He mourned over Jerusalem and the people's lack of belief in Him. He wanted to gather the people together as a hen gathers her brood under her wings, but the people weren't willing (see Matthew 23:37 and Luke 13:34). He understood our mom-felt desire to draw our precious ones close.

We can relate to each of these roles because we've filled them ourselves with our children. What a wonderful thing it is to realize that God experiences the same depth of nurturing and protection toward us!

• •

Dear Lord, I know You'll do anything to protect me and show me love because I do the same for my children. Thank You for caring enough to love me not just as our Father but also as a mother. Amen.

Staying Centered

As a deer longs for streams of water,
so I long for You, God.
PSALM 42:1 HCSB

Jeanne is an elementary school principal who's about to go through a big transition as a mom. Her youngest child will be moving to middle school next year, and it will be the first time in almost ten years that she won't have one of her children nearby. She doesn't see her children every day at school and is normally too busy with work to think about what they're doing in class. But on days when things are unusually hectic or stressful, she tries to steal a few minutes to visit the cafeteria while one of them is eating lunch.

"I don't always sit and visit," she says. "Some days they're having so much fun with friends that I don't want to interrupt. But just seeing their smiles or being able to walk by and squeeze a shoulder makes a difference. It reminds me why I'm here. It centers me." We all need reminders of why we do the things we do as moms and friends and employees. We need a touch point that keeps us grounded.

Maybe we're like Jeanne and find our focal point in our children. Maybe we visit a special place because it helps us

relax. Whatever tangible reminders we might have, our true centering place is with God.

Stepping away from the world to spend time with God can calm our spirit, ease our fears, and give us much-needed encouragement. We can soak up God's love like a deer drinking fresh water (see Psalm 42:1). We can renew our strength for what lies ahead (see Isaiah 40:31). Even if we spend time with God and don't say a word, He knows exactly what we need (see Romans 8:26). Busy lives need centering points more than ever. We're blessed to have God as ours.

• •

Lord, thank You for being my centering point, the place where I can come to help make sense of everything else. Renew me and strengthen me for this day. Amen.

A Special Name

*"I will give to each one a white stone, and on the
stone will be engraved a new name that no one
understands except the one who receives it."*
REVELATION 2:17 NLT

A name is one of the most important gifts we give our babies, the main identifier they'll have throughout their lives. Picking that perfect name is no easy task and one we don't take lightly. Once we make a decision, we start looking for things that incorporate our child's name. Towels, bibs, and decorative plaques for our babies later give way to key chains, T-shirts, and monogrammed luggage. We want our children to be proud of the names we chose.

Stories throughout the Bible tell of how people acquired their names and what the names mean. There is also a special promise in Revelation 2:17 that says Jesus will give each of us a white stone with a new name on it, a name known only to us. What's the big deal about a rock? The fact that it includes a new, special name that's so personal no one else knows it. It will be a secret known only to two people—that person and Jesus. And it's a name that Jesus picks especially for us because He knows everything about us from the time in our mother's

womb until the day we meet Him in heaven.

There's no way to know yet what our new names will be or how Jesus will select them. We don't know if those names will reflect our personalities, symbolize accomplishments we've made, or be totally unrelated to our lives on earth. But when we do learn that special name, when we hear Jesus say it for the first time, we'll know that He spent time choosing the perfect new name for us just like we spent time choosing our own children's names. That should make us all feel cherished and special.

• •

Dear Lord, thank You for the white stone with my special new name...a name that perfectly reflects Your love for me and the relationship we have. I can hardly wait to learn what it is someday. Amen.

DAY 97

What's to Come

He anointed us, set his seal of ownership on us,
and put his Spirit in our hearts as a deposit,
guaranteeing what is to come.
2 CORINTHIANS 1:21–22 NIV

Countless jokes and real-life stories circulate about the incessant questions kids ask on road trips: "Where are we going?" "Are we there yet?" "How much longer?" They wear our patience thin and might make us question our sanity. It's nice to know we don't have to ask the same questions about our journey with God.

Learning to walk through every day with faith is an ongoing process. Every day is a chance for us to learn and grow and become better women for God. It's a chance to be an even better mom to our children than we were the day before. The process starts when we accept God into our lives and He claims us as His own. Having God's Spirit within our hearts gives us a small taste of what's to come—eternity in heaven with God. It's like the down payment we make to reserve our favorite vacation spot, giving us a glimpse of what's to come so that we can look forward to getting there.

There's also another way we can think about the things to

come. When we know that something different is waiting for us, we're acknowledging that the place we're in right now isn't permanent. Something will be changing. In terms of our faith, that "something" is where we're meant to live. As Christians, we're guaranteed eternal life in heaven—the best possible "what is to come" imaginable.

On those days when the world is crashing all around us, the kids are asking too many questions, and heaven seems so far away, we can hold on to that promise of heaven and know that things will get better. We have the Holy Spirit within us to prove it and remind us where we're heading.

· ·

Thank You, Lord, for claiming me and for holding a spot for me in heaven. Use Your Spirit to remind me that even though every day won't be perfect here, I'm working toward eternal perfection with You. Amen.

Bubbles and Butterflies

*For you created my inmost being; you knit me
together in my mother's womb. I praise you
because I am fearfully and wonderfully made;
your works are wonderful, I know that full well.*
PSALM 139:13–14 NIV

Every newly expectant mom asks the same question of other
moms at some point: how will it feel when the baby moves for
the first time? That question and the memories that come with
it probably bring a smile to our faces. What's a good answer?
Maybe saying it felt like butterflies or bubbles floating inside
us. Or a little tap, tap, tap as if the baby was making sure
we knew someone was there. Perhaps a slight tickle or
muscle spasm unlike any we'd experienced before.

Isn't it amazing that we can feel something that small inside
us? What a gift, that God allows us to have those weeks of
connection all to ourselves before anyone else can see or feel
our baby's movements. God wants us to have that same sort of
connection with Him—one that comes from deep within and is
unlike anything we've ever experienced. Our relationship isn't
something we should be ashamed to tell people about, but it's
also okay to savor parts of it just for ourselves.

We can tell God our most intimate secrets, craziest dreams, and debilitating fears. We can share our funniest moments, explosive rages, and biggest celebrations. Each one strengthens our relationship with Him and makes God a more integral part of our daily lives.

Our child might be a newborn or toddler stealing our sleep, a teenager keeping us exasperated, or an adult facing the real world. Whatever our phase of motherhood, let's close our eyes and remember that first movement that was so tiny we wondered if we were imagining it. Marvel again at the miracle of creation. And finally, let's thank God once more for the privilege of sharing in that joy—and the way it can remind us of our connection with God.

• •

Dear God, I'm amazed whenever I think of how You make us with such care, each tiny part at exactly the right time. Thank You for creating life in me. Help me to always remember it with awe and thanksgiving and as a reminder of my connection with You. Amen.

203

Sleeping Beauties

When Aaron and all the Israelites saw Moses, his face
was radiant, and they were afraid to come near him.
EXODUS 34:30 NIV

Sleep plays strange games with our children. We put them to bed knowing exactly how old they are and how they look. But sometimes as we watch them later, or in the morning when we go to wake them, we see glimpses beyond the reality of that day.

A flash of expression on our teenager's face takes us back to the toddler years when eyelashes brushed chubby cheeks and belly laughs were a daily occurrence. Then, just as quickly, we see their features as an adult, with refined jawlines and stronger noses. It's enough to snatch our breath away and remind us once again how fleeting this life really is. How fragile these bodies might appear but how resilient they are because of God's strength within.

Maybe this is how God sees us—as the woman of our past, present, and future, all mingled together. A girl who grows to be a woman and mom who will do anything necessary for her family. A woman who sometimes wonders how she'll survive a situation yet manages to pull through by clinging to God.

Most importantly, we hope that God sees us as women who run after Him with a desire to deepen their faith.

The Bible tells of a time when Moses climbed a mountain to meet with God. When he returned to the people below, Moses' face was so radiant from being in God's presence that the people were afraid to come near him. They made him cover his face (see Exodus 34:29–35). What an amazing sight to see, all because Moses spent time with God. Our faces undoubtedly change over the years just as our children's do. Let's ask God to draw us closer to Him so that we can reflect that same love Moses did.

● ●

Dear God, I want to love You so much and be so close to You that it shines on my face like it did for Moses. Show me how to take those steps and draw others closer to You. Thank You. Amen.

Unforgettable You

*Behold, I have engraved you on the palms of my
hands; your walls are continually before me.*
ISAIAH 49:16 ESV

Engraving is one way to make a gift special, no matter our child's
age. From silver baby cups and lockets to crystal stemware as
a wedding gift, engraving a name or monogram marks that
object as our child's forever. God shows that we belong to Him
in the same way.

The Bible says that God engraves us on the palms of His
hands. This is far beyond standard writing; *Webster's* definition
of engraving is "to impress deeply or permanently on the mind
or memory, as though by engraving." When God engraves our
name, it's there to stay. It's not written with marker or pen like
a reminder we might leave ourselves.

And notice where our name is written. The palm is one of
the most sensitive parts of our body, so having our name on
God's palm means we're in a special place. The palm also is one
body part that we use—and see—constantly. God writes our
names there so we're easy to notice and remember.

Some translations of Isaiah 49:16 use the word *inscribed*
instead of *engraved*. The meaning is basically the same, although

Webster's definition of inscribed includes an interesting phrase: "to add the name of someone to a list." When we accept Jesus as our Savior, the Bible says our names are written in the Book of Life along with all those who have believed the same thing, whether they were international evangelists, neighborhood pastors, or ordinary women like us just trying to be the best moms they could be.

What an encouragement! No matter how bad our day might be or how far off track we might get, our names are still there—permanently engraved—on the palm of God's hand. God is still caring about us and claiming us as His.

• •

Dear Lord, it's hard to believe that You care for me so much that You engrave my name on the palm of Your hand. Thank You for always loving me and never forgetting me. Amen.

Looking for More Encouragement for Your Heart?

Worry Less, Pray More

This purposeful devotional guide features 180 readings and prayers designed to help alleviate your worries as you learn to live in the peace of the almighty God, who offers calm for your anxiety-filled soul.

Paperback / 978-1-68322-861-5

Too Blessed to be Stressed: 3-Minute Devotions for Women

You'll find the spiritual pick-me-up you need in *Too Blessed to Be Stressed: 3-Minute Devotions for Women.* This book from bestselling author Debora M. Coty packs a powerful dose of inspiration, encouragement, humor, and faith into 180 just-right-sized readings for your busy schedule.

Paperback / 978-1-63409-569-3